Simplify Testing with React Testing Library

Create maintainable tests using RTL that do not break with changes

Scottie Crump

BIRMINGHAM—MUMBAI

Simplify Testing with React Testing Library

Publishing Product Manager: Aaron Tanna

Senior Editor: Hayden Edwards

Content Development Editor: Abhishek Jadhav

Technical Editor: Deepesh Patel

Copy Editor: Safis Editing

Project Coordinator: Manthan Patel

Proofreader: Safis Editing

Indexer: Rekha Nair

Production Designer: Prashant Ghare

First published: April 2021

Production reference: 1160421

Published by Packt Publishing Ltd.

Livery Place

35 Livery Street

Birmingham

B3 2PB, UK.

ISBN 978-1-80056-445-9

www.packt.com

To my mother, Judy, and father, Randall, for always being there and encouraging me to be the best at whatever my heart desires. To my wife, Victoria, for being my loving partner and being patient enough to allow me to work countless hours on this project while holding back the urge to throw my laptop out of the window.

To my son, Liam, my greatest motivator, who gave me the extra energy to stay up late at night to write another sentence and line of code.

– Scottie Crump

Contributors

About the author

Scottie Crump is a senior test engineer with over four years' experience as
a consultant working with clients from a variety of sectors, including automotive,
retail, telecommunications, and healthcare, among others. Scottie has also worked with
numerous students looking to break into the software industry at Coding Bootcamp
settings. His background in quality and software engineering and education enables him
to be a crucial cog in any client's project. Scottie has helped bring industry best practices
and data-driven insights to support key business objectives.

About the reviewer

Alexander Krolick is an open source maintainer of React Testing Library and related projects.

Table of Contents

3

Testing Complex Components with React Testing Library

4

Integration Testing and Third-Party Libraries in Your Application

7
End-to-End UI Testing with Cypress

Answers

Other Books You May Enjoy

Index

Preface

React Testing Library (RTL) is a lightweight and easy-to-use tool for testing the Document Object Model (DOM) output of components. This book will show you how to utilize this modern, user-friendly tool to test React components, explaining its benefits to reduce risk in React applications.

The book demonstrates code snippets that will allow you to implement RTL with ease, helping you understand the guiding principles of the DOM Testing Library to write tests from the user's perspective. You'll explore the advantages of testing components from the perspective of individuals who will actually use your components, and you'll use Test-Driven Development (TDD) to drive the process of writing tests. As you advance, you'll discover how to add RTL to React projects, test components using the Context API, and also learn how to write UI end-to-end tests using the popular Cypress library. Throughout this book, you'll work with practical examples and useful explanations to be able to confidently create tests that don't break when changes are made.

By the end of this React book, you will have learned all you need to be able to test React components with ease.

Who this book is for?

This book is for software engineers, quality engineers and React developers who want to learn about modern practices used for testing React components using the latest testing tool, RTL. Basic knowledge of React development is required to get the most out of this book..

What this book covers?

Chapter 1, *Exploring React Testing Library*, will help you understand the guiding principles of the DOM Testing Library to write tests from the perspective of the user. You will learn the disadvantages of implementing detail-focused testing. Finally, you will learn the advantages of using jest-dom to enhance our tests using RTL.

Chapter 2, *Working with React Testing Library*, will teach you how to add RTL to React projects. You will learn how to properly structure tests using the API. You will look at presentational components and write some initial tests. Finally, we will learn how to use the debug method to assist us in the process of writing tests.

Chapter 3, Testing Complex Components with React Testing Library, will help you understand how to test more complex React components. You will learn how to simulate user interactions with Fire Event and the user event module. You will learn how to use TDD to drive the process of writing tests. Finally, you will unit test components that interact with APIs.

Chapter 4, Integration Testing and Third-Party Libraries in Your Application, teaches you how to test components in various React applications. You will learn how to test integrated components and how to test components using the Context API. Finally, you will test components using popular third-party libraries such as GraphQL and Redux.

Chapter 5, Refactoring Legacy Applications with React Testing Library, will teach you strategies for dealing with breaking changes while refactoring legacy React applications. You will learn how to update production packages while using RTL tests to guide you in resolving breaking changes. You will also learn how to convert tests written in Enzyme or ReactTestUtils to RTL.

Chapter 6, Implementing Additional Tools and Plugins for Testing, will help you learn additional tools to enhance your ability to test React applications using RTL.

Chapter 7, End-To-End UI Testing with Cypress, will teach you how to write end-to-end UI tests using the popular Cypress library. You will learn design patterns to structure your tests. You will learn how to test APIs with Cypress. Finally, you will learn how to integrate Cucumber and React Developer Tools into your test suite.

To get the most out of this book

You will need NodeJS and npm installed on your computer—the latest versions, if possible. All code examples have been tested using RTL version 11.2.5 on macOS Big Sur version 11.2.3. However, they should work with future version releases too.

Software/hardware covered in the book	OS requirements
React 17	Windows, macOS, and Linux (Any)
React Testing Library 11.2.5	Windows, macOS, and Linux (Any)
Jest-dom 5.11.9	Windows, macOS, and Linux (Any)
user-event 13.0.7	Windows, macOS, and Linux (Any)
Material-UI 4.11.3	Windows, macOS, and Linux (Any)
Mock Service Worker 0.27.1	Windows, macOS, and Linux (Any)
Apollo Client 3.3.12	Windows, macOS, and Linux (Any)
Redux Toolkit 1.5.0	Windows, macOS, and Linux (Any)
Cypress 6.8.0	Windows, macOS, and Linux (Any)
Cypress Testing Library 7.0.4	Windows, macOS, and Linux (Any)
Cypress Cucumber Preprocessor 4.0.3	Windows, macOS, and Linux (Any)

You are free to use any code editor for chapter examples. However, suggested extensions to enhance your experience when running examples are provided for the VSCode editor.

If you are using the digital version of this book, we advise you to type the code yourself or access the code via the GitHub repository (link available in the next section). Doing so will help you avoid any potential errors related to copy/pasting of code.

Download the example code files

You can download the example code files for this book from your account at www.packt.com. If you purchased this book elsewhere, you can visit www.packtpub.com/support and register to have the files emailed directly to you.

You can download the code files by following these steps:

1. Log in or register at www.packt.com.
2. Select the **Support** tab.
3. Click on **Code Downloads**.
4. Enter the name of the book in the **Search** box and follow the onscreen instructions.

Once the file is downloaded, please make sure that you unzip or extract the folder using the latest version of:

- WinRAR/7-Zip for Windows

- Zipeg/iZip/UnRarX for Mac

- 7-Zip/PeaZip for Linux

The code bundle for the book is also hosted on GitHub at `https://github.com/PacktPublishing/Simplify-Testing-with-React-Testing-Library`. In case there's an update to the code, it will be updated on the existing GitHub repository.

We also have other code bundles from our rich catalog of books and videos available at `https://github.com/PacktPublishing/`. Check them out!

Download the color images

We also provide a PDF file that has color images of the screenshots/diagrams used in this book. You can download it here: `https://static.packt-cdn.com/downloads/9781800564459_ColorImages.pdf`.

Conventions used

There are a number of text conventions used throughout this book.

`Code in text`: Indicates code words in text, database table names, folder names, filenames, file extensions, pathnames, dummy URLs, user input, and Twitter handles. Here is an example: "Mount the downloaded `WebStorm-10*.dmg` disk image file as another disk in your system."

A block of code is set as follows:

```
html, body, #map {
  height: 100%;
  margin: 0;
  padding: 0
}
```

When we wish to draw your attention to a particular part of a code block, the relevant lines or items are set in bold:

```
[default]
exten => s,1,Dial(Zap/1|30)
exten => s,2,Voicemail(u100)
exten => s,102,Voicemail(b100)
exten => i,1,Voicemail(s0)
```

Any command-line input or output is written as follows:

```
$ mkdir css
$ cd css
```

Bold: Indicates a new term, an important word, or words that you see onscreen. For example, words in menus or dialog boxes appear in the text like this. Here is an example: "Select **System info** from the **Administration** panel."

> **Tips or important notes**
> Appear like this.

Get in touch

Feedback from our readers is always welcome.

General feedback: If you have questions about any aspect of this book, mention the book title in the subject of your message and email us at customercare@packtpub.com.

Errata: Although we have taken every care to ensure the accuracy of our content, mistakes do happen. If you have found a mistake in this book, we would be grateful if you would report this to us. Please visit www.packtpub.com/support/errata, selecting your book, clicking on the Errata Submission Form link, and entering the details.

Piracy: If you come across any illegal copies of our works in any form on the Internet, we would be grateful if you would provide us with the location address or website name. Please contact us at copyright@packt.com with a link to the material.

If you are interested in becoming an author: If there is a topic that you have expertise in and you are interested in either writing or contributing to a book, please visit authors.packtpub.com.

Reviews

Please leave a review. Once you have read and used this book, why not leave a review on the site that you purchased it from? Potential readers can then see and use your unbiased opinion to make purchase decisions, we at Packt can understand what you think about our products, and our authors can see your feedback on their book. Thank you!

For more information about Packt, please visit `packt.com`.

1

Exploring React Testing Library

React Testing Library is a modern tool for testing the UI output of React components. It abstracts a lot of boilerplate code, allowing you to write code that is easier to read, and allows you to test the code. The library encourages you to move away from testing implementation details, to avoid many false negative and false positive test cases. Instead, the library's API of tools makes it easy for you to write tests that simulate actual users' behaviors with your components, yielding confidence that the application works as expected for users. Also, because the library urges you to focus on the user when writing tests, you don't need to continuously update tests that fail when you refactor the code's implementation details. The React Testing Library allows you to write tests that fail when critical functionality unexpectedly changes, thus providing more value.

By the end of this chapter, you will understand what the implementation details are and the disadvantages they bring regarding maintenance and value in your test cases. For many years, it has been common for teams to test their components by focusing on the code's implementation details. Many teams still use this approach today. However, there are better ways to test the components that we will cover in this chapter. You will learn how to add confidence to your test case planning by understanding how to shift your thinking toward testing from the user's perspective. We will introduce you to the ideas behind the **Document Object Model (DOM)** Testing Library to ease the task of testing before transitioning to the primary focus, the React version of the library.

Next, you will learn about the Jest testing framework, tasked with executing and asserting our tests' output. Finally, you will learn how to install and use the `jest-dom` utility to enhance test assertions.

In this chapter, we're going to cover the following main topics:

- Learning about the DOM Testing Library
- Understanding the role of Jest in testing React applications
- Learning about the advantages of using `jest-dom` to test React applications with Jest
- Understanding the disadvantages of implementation detail-focused testing

The lessons of this chapter will set the foundation for understanding how you will use React Testing Library throughout this book to write better tests that focus on the user's perspective. The skills gained in this chapter will help whether you are new to writing tests for React applications or are an experienced tester looking for better ways to verify that your code works as expected.

Technical requirements

For the examples in this chapter, you will need to have Node.js installed on your machine. You can find the code examples for this chapter here: `https://github.com/ PacktPublishing/Simplify-Testing-with-React-Testing-Library/ tree/master/Chapter01`.

Introducing the DOM Testing Library

The **DOM Testing Library** is a collection of tools created by Kent C. Dodds and numerous contributors to make our lives easier when our goal is to test our applications' UI from real users' perspectives. This section will give you an overview of how the library can help make testing efforts focused on users' perspectives a lot easier.

What is the DOM Testing Library?

The DOM Testing Library makes it easier to test the UI of applications like real users to gain confidence that the application works as expected for users. There are no methods to get the component's state value or directly invoke component methods.

The library encourages you to select DOM elements in ways that are available to all users. The library's API includes accessibility-focused query methods allowing you to interact with the DOM like users with disabilities who require tools such as screen readers or other forms of assistive technology to navigate applications. For example, say you want to select the following element in your test:

```
<input
    type="text"
    id="firstname"
    placeholder="first name..."
>
```

In the preceding code, we have an input element of type `"text"`. You could select the input on the screen by its placeholder value of `"First Name..."` with the DOM Testing Library like so:

```
screen.getByPlaceholderText(/first name/i)
```

The `getByPlaceholderText` method is used from the screen object to select the DOM element by its placeholder value in the preceding code. The screen object allows you to select elements attached to the body element of the DOM. Notice the regular expression used in the query. It is doubtful that a user would care if the text were in upper or lowercase, so the DOM Testing Library allows you to search for elements by text values regardless of the case.

Having the ability to select elements by text value regardless of their case increases the test's ability to maintain a passing result despite changes to implementation details of the element. The use of the `getByPlaceholderText` method is a great way to select elements, but we can be even more specific by refactoring the source code:

```
<label for="firstname">First name:</label>
<input
    type="text"
    id="firstname"
    name="firstname"
    placeholder="first name..."
>
```

In the preceding code, we added a `label` element and an accessible `name` attribute to the input. Now all users, including those using screen readers, can access the element. We can select the input element in our test like so:

```
screen.getByRole('textbox', {
  name: /first name:/i
})
```

In the preceding code, we use the `getByRole` method to select the element by its role of a textbox with the name `first name`. Selecting an element by its role is the preferred way to select elements with the DOM Testing Library when available.

The library is very flexible in that you can use it with any JavaScript test runner, such as Mocha or Jest, that provides APIs to access the DOM. We will run our tests with Jest in this book and learn more about it in the next section. There are many specific versions of the DOM Testing Library for popular UI frameworks and libraries.

The particular versions add extra features to the DOM Testing Library's API for more comfortable use. For example, to place a React component under test into the DOM, we can use the `render` method of `ReactDOM` to place the component into an element attached to the DOM:

```
const div = document.createElement('div');
ReactDOM.render(<SomeComponent />, div);
document.body.appendChild(div);
screen.getByText('Login');
```

In the preceding code, first, we create a `div` element. Next, we attach `SomeComponent` to the `div` element. Then, we attach `div` to the `body` element of the DOM. Finally, we use the `getByText` method of the DOM Testing Library's `screen` object to find an element with the text value of `Login`. If we use React Testing Library, we can replace the first three lines from the preceding code with the `render` method:

```
render(<SomeComponent />);
```

In the preceding code, we use React Testing Library's `render` method to automatically render the component under test into the DOM for us. We will show you how to use the React version of the library throughout this book. There is even support for many popular end-to-end testing frameworks, such as Cypress (`https://www.cypress.io/`), which we will cover in *Chapter 7, End-to-End UI Testing with Cypress*. The library provides a utility to enhance test assertions with Jest, which we will cover later in this chapter.

Next, we will cover the guiding principles behind the DOM Testing Library.

Guiding principles

The DOM Testing Library is driven by providing easy-to-use APIs to test your rendered applications in the DOM. The tools help give you confidence that your tests represent actions that actual users are likely to take. For example, you might build an email form allowing customers to subscribe to your newsletter such as the following:

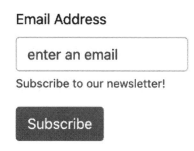

Figure 1.1 – Subscription form component

Because you want to be sure that the form works, you'll think about the steps a potential subscriber would take while interacting with the form. You think to yourself, *If I were a user, first, I might look for a label named Email Address or a placeholder that has the text "enter an email."* The DOM Testing Library has a method called getByLabelText to quickly find the email input by the label displayed on the screen. The DOM Testing Library has another method called getByPlaceholderText that allows you to locate an input via its placeholder value.

After entering the email, you think to yourself, *Next, I would look for a button with the text "Subscribe" and click it.* The DOM Testing Library provides a method called getByText that allows you to find a button by its text value. Also, the library provides a method called getByRole that enables you to query the DOM specifically for an element with the role of button with the subscribe text value.

Now that you understand the DOM Testing Library's general concepts, we will discuss the framework we will use to execute our test cases in the next section.

Executing test cases with Jest

Jest is a JavaScript testing framework created by the team at Facebook. In this section, we will cover a brief overview of Jest and how we can use it to verify the output of test cases for React components.

Running tests with Jest

Most React projects are tested with Jest, so it makes sense to introduce this tool alongside learning React Testing Library. When we write our tests using React Testing Library, we need a test runner to execute the test.

Use the following command to install Jest in your project:

```
npm install --save-dev jest
```

We will run our React tests using Jest. At a high level, Jest provides the `describe`, `it`, `test`, and `expect` functions to organize and execute tests. You can think of the `describe` function as a test suite. Use the `describe` function to group related tests for specific components. The `it` and `test` functions are for specific tests. The `it` and `test` functions are interchangeable functions used to house and run the code for individual test cases. Use the `expect` function to assert the expected output. Jest also provides mock functions to handle code outside the realm of tests and coverage reporting. A test written with Jest can be as simple as testing the output of a pure function.

In the following example, we use the `test` and `expect` functions to assert the total number of characters in a provided name:

```
test('should return the total number of characters', () => {
  function totalCharsInName(name) {
    return name.length;
  }
  expect(totalCharsInName('Steve')).toEqual(5);
});
```

Let's look at an example test that will assert the details of a `Profile` component created with a class-style React component. The `Profile` component accepts employee information and displays it as a card-style element in the DOM. A user can click a button to hide or show the employee's details on the screen. Here is a screenshot of the component's DOM output:

Steve Williams

Software Engineer III

Hide Details

I love building with React!

Figure 1.2 – Profile component

Let's take a look at the code for the Profile component. We create a state object with the showDetails property initially set to true. Next, we create a setDetails method that will update the state value of showDetails:

```
import React, { Component } from 'react';


export default class Profile extends Component {
  state = { showDetails: true };
  setDetails = () => {
    this.setState((prevState) => ({ showDetails: !prevState.
      showDetails }));
  };
```

Inside the render method, we display the name and title properties passed into the component:

```
render() {
    return (
        <div className="card" style={{ width: "18rem" }}>
          <img
            className="card-img-top"
            src="http://fakeimg.pl/286x180?font=lobster"
            alt="Card cap"
          />
          <div className="card-body">
```

```
<h5 className="card-title">{this.props.name}</h5>
<p className="card-subtitle mb-2 text-muted">{this.
    props.title}</p>
```

Note that the src image just has a placeholder image, but ideally would accept a passed-in value such as the name and title property values.

Lastly, we have a button that invokes the setDetails method when clicked. The button's text is set to either Hide Details or Display Details based on the value of state.showDetails. Also, the employee details are displayed based on the value of state.showDetails:

```
button onClick={this.setDetails} className="btn btn-primary">
          {this.state.showDetails ? "Hide Details" : "Display
              Details"}
        </button>
        {this.state.showDetails ? (
          <p className="card-text details">{this.props.
              details}</p>
        ) : null}
      </div>
    </div>
  );
  }
}
```

Now, let's look at the code for a Profile component test that verifies the button with the text "display details" is shown when the button with the text "hide details" is clicked:

```
test('Profile, given click "hide details" button, shows
 "display details" button', () => {
  const div = document.createElement('div');
  ReactDOM.render(
    <Profile
      name='John Doe'
      title='Team Lead'
      details='This is my 5th year and I love helping others'
    />,
    div
```

```
  );
document.body.appendChild(div);
```

In the preceding code, we create a div element to later use with the component under test. Next, we use the render method of ReactDOM to render the Profile component with passed-in properties into div. Finally, we add div with the component to the body element of the DOM. Next, we perform actions on the resulting DOM output:

```
const hideDetailsBtn = screen.getByRole('button', { name: /
    hide details/i });


fireEvent.click(hideDetailsBtn);
const displayDetailsBtn = screen.getByRole('button', {
    name: /display details/i,
});
```

In the preceding code, first we grab the button with the name hide details. Next, we fire a click event on the hide details button. Then, we grab the button with the name display details. Next, we will make assertions:

```
expect(displayDetailsBtn).toBeTruthy();
// Test cleanup
    div.remove();
});
```

In the preceding code, first, we expect the display details button to be *truthy*, meaning the element is found in the DOM. Then, we do some test cleanup by removing div from the DOM's body element, allowing successive tests to start from a clean slate.

Let's look at the previous test again by focusing on the Jest parts of the code.

All the code for a specific test lives inside an it or test method:

```
test(Profile, given click "hide details" button, shows "display
    details" button', () => {}
it(Profile, given click "hide details" button, shows "display
    details" button', () => {}
```

This method and others in the test file will execute when Jest is run with the **Node Package Manager** (npm) test. Jest will find your test file, execute tests within it, and show the test results in the console:

```
PASS  src/ProfileDOMTestingLib.test.js
 ✓ Profile, given click "hide details" button, shows "display details" button (75ms)

Test Suites: 1 passed, 1 total
Tests:       1 passed, 1 total
Snapshots:   0 total
Time:        2.01s
Ran all test suites matching /src\/ProfileDOMTestingLib\.test\.js/i.
```

Figure 1.3 – Profile test passed console output

If we had multiple tests for a component, we could organize them together in the `describe` method:

```
describe(<Profile />, () => {
  test(given click "hide details" button, shows "display
    details" button', () => {}
  test('another test for the profile component', () => {}
}
```

The most important part of a test is the assertion. In Jest, you can assert the output of the test using the `expect` method:

```
expect(displayDetailsBtn).toBeTruthy();
```

The `toBeTruthy` method chained off the `expect` method is one of many matcher methods that Jest provides to verify the expected result of the code passed into `expect`.

Now you understand the role Jest plays in testing React applications. You can install the framework and use its API to organize, write, and execute test cases. Next, you will learn about a utility provided by the Testing Library to add enhanced Jest assertion matchers to help with testing React components.

Enhancing Jest assertions with jest-dom

`jest-dom` is a utility tool from the DOM Testing Library that provides extra Jest assertions to use in tests. In this section, you will learn how to install `jest-dom` and understand the advantages of using `jest-dom` with Jest.

Adding jest-dom to a project

Add jest-dom to a project that includes Jest using the following steps:

1. Install the package using npm:

    ```
    npm install --save-dev @testing-library/jest-dom
    ```

2. Add the following snippet to the top of your test file:

    ```
    import '@testing-library/jest-dom/extend-expect';
    ```

After installing and importing jest-dom into your test file, you can start using the extra assertions as they are now chained off the expect method. You will see detailed illustrated use cases in the next section.

Advantages of using jest-dom with Jest

You can enhance user-focused testing goals by including jest-dom in React projects that use Jest. jest-dom provides two significant enhancements for Jest assertions. First, jest-dom provides over 20 custom DOM matchers that create more descriptive test code. Second, jest-dom also provides better context-specific error messages. We will show you examples of both advantages in the following subsections.

jest-dom descriptive test code examples

To illustrate the benefits of using jest-dom, first, we will revisit our Profile component test file from the previous section, *Introducing the DOM Testing Library*. Note that we will only focus on the assertion code in the test. We asserted the text value of an element:

```
const displayDetailsBtn = screen.getByRole('button', {
    name: /display details/i,
});
expect(displayDetailsBtn).toBeTruthy();
```

The syntax of the previous code may not be as clear to some developers who are unfamiliar with the code base. It may not be evident that we are verifying the element is found in the DOM. jest-dom has a toBeInTheDocument() method to provide a more straightforward syntax.

Next, we will refactor our code using use the `jest-dom` `toBeInTheDocument()` method to make the code more descriptive:

```
expect(displayDetailsBtn).toBeInTheDocument();
```

Now, from the syntax it is more apparent that we are expecting the element to be in the DOM. We could also assert that the `hide details` button is removed from the DOM when clicked:

```
const removedHideDetailsBtn = screen.queryByRole('button',
  {
    name: /hide details/i,
  });
expect(removedHideDetailsBtn).toBeFalsy();
```

Jest's `toBeFalsy()` method was used to return a `null` value, which evaluates to `false` in JavaScript. For the test, this means the element was not found in the DOM. However, the syntax is not clear that using `toBeFalsy()` indicates the element wasn't found in the DOM as expected and may confuse some developers looking at the code.

We can use the `toBeInTheDocument()` method again to provide a more straightforward syntax:

```
expect(removedHideDetailsBtn).not.toBeInTheDocument();
```

Now, from the syntax in the previous code it is more apparent that we expect the element to not be in the DOM. Notice that Jest's `not` property is used before the `jest-dom` method. The `not` property is used to return the opposite value. If we did not use the `not` property, we would be asserting the element is in the DOM.

For another example, let's say we have the following login form we want to test:

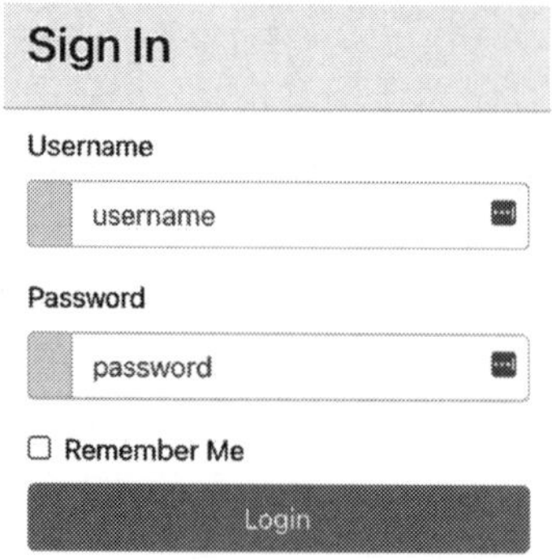

Figure 1.4 – Login component

In the previous screenshot, we have a login form feature that allows a user to enter a username and password and check a **Remember Me** checkbox. The **Login** button starts out in a `disabled` state until the user enters values for the `username` and `password` fields. The login form in this example is currently still in development, so at the moment, nothing happens when a user clicks the **Login** button. However, we can write a test to verify the functionality of the **Login** button being enabled when a user enters credentials:

```
test('Login, given credentials, returns enabled submit button',
() => {
  const div = document.createElement('div');
  ReactDOM.render(<Login />, div);
  document.body.appendChild(div);
  const username = screen.getByRole('textbox', { name: /
    username/i });
  const password = screen.getByLabelText(/password/i);
  const rememberMe = screen.getByRole('checkbox');
  const loginBtn = screen.getByRole('button', { name: /submit/i
});
```

In the preceding code, we set up our test by rendering the `Login` component into the `div` tag and attaching it to the `body` element in the DOM. Next, we grab all the form elements, which include the `username`, `password`, `rememberMe`, and `login` buttons, and place them in variables.

Next, we will perform user actions on the DOM:

```
const fakeData = {
  username: 'test user',
  password: '123password',
};
fireEvent.change(username, { target: { value: fakeData.
  username } });
fireEvent.change(password, { target: { value: fakeData.
  password } });
fireEvent.click(rememberMe);
```

In the preceding code, we create a `fakeData` object with values to use in the test. Next, we use `fireEvent` to add values to the `username` and `password` fields and finally, to click the `rememberMe` checkbox. Next, we will make assertions:

```
expect(loginBtn.hasAttribute('disabled')).toBe(false);
```

In the preceding code, we assert that `loginBtn` has a `disabled` attribute set to `false`. However, we can use a `jest-dom` assertion method for a cleaner syntax:

```
expect(loginBtn).not.toBeDisabled()
```

In the preceding code, we use the `toBeDisabled()` method to verify the **Login** button is not disabled in a more straightforward syntax. We can also use `jest-dom` methods to verify the expected state of the form after entering values:

```
expect(screen.getByTestId('form')).toHaveFormValues({
    username: fakeData.username,
    password: fakeData.password,
    rememberMe: true,
});
```

In the preceding code, we use the `toHaveFormValues()` method to verify the form inputs have the entered `fakeData` values using an easy-to-read syntax. The great thing about our previous test is that as long as the functionality stays the same, we can continue building out the login form or refactor the internal code without concerns that our current tests will break.

Now you understand how `jest-dom` methods allow you to write more descriptive test code. Next, we will use the same examples to illustrate how `jest-dom` methods provide better context-specific error messages.

jest-dom error message example

In the previous section, we asserted that the **Login** button was not disabled after a user entered the `username` and `password` credentials for the `Login` component. We could have also asserted that the **Login** button is disabled before a user enters credentials. Before using the enhanced `jest-dom assertion` method, we could have mistakenly typed `disable` instead of `disabled` in the `hasAttribute` method:

```
expect(loginBtn.hasAttribute('disable')).toBe(true);
fireEvent.change(username, { target: { value: fakeData.username
} });
fireEvent.change(password, { target: { value: fakeData.password
} });
```

The typo in the previous code would lead to the following test result output:

```
● Login, given credentials, returns enabled submit button

  expect(received).toBe(expected) // Object.is equality

  Expected: true
  Received: false

        const loginBtn = screen.getByRole('button', { name: /submit/i });

  >       expect(loginBtn.hasAttribute('disable')).toBe(true);
                                                    ^
```

Figure 1.5 – Login component false negative test

In the previous screenshot, the results indicate the test failed from receiving a false value at the point where we expect the **Login** button to be disabled and return a result of `true`. The result is a false negative because the source code was correct, but our test code was incorrect.

The error message does not make it obvious that the assertion code had a typo causing our test not to receive the expected result. We could make a similar test code error by mistakenly using the `not` property with the `jest-dom` `toBeDisabled` method:

```
expect(loginBtn).not.toBeDisabled();
fireEvent.change(username, { target: { value: fakeData.username
} });
fireEvent.change(password, { target: { value: fakeData.password
} });
fireEvent.click(rememberMe);
```

In the previous code, we mistakenly assert the **Login** button is not disabled at the point in the test when it should be disabled. The test code mistake in the previous code would lead to the following test result output:

```
FAIL  src/Login.test.js
  × Login, given credentials, returns enabled submit button (104ms)

  ● Login, given credentials, returns enabled submit button

    expect(element).not.toBeDisabled()

    Received element is disabled:
      <input class="btn btn-primary w-100" disabled="" type="submit" value="Login" />
```

Figure 1.6 – Second login component false negative test

In the previous screenshot, the results indicate the test fails, but we also receive helpful feedback for pinpointing the error while debugging. The test output informs us that the received element is disabled and logs the element to the console to view all the attributes. The `disabled` attribute is shown in the `element` output, which helps us understand that we need to debug our test code to know why we didn't receive the expected result.

Now you know how `jest-dom`'s methods provide better context-specific error messages to resolve issues faster. In the next section, we will learn about the disadvantages of including implementation details in our tests.

Testing implementation details

Implementation details include the component state's current value or explicitly invoking a method attached to a button in the DOM. Implementation details are the *under-the-hood* parts of components abstracted away from the user when they use the component. As an analogy, we can think of the experience of driving a car. To move, you must use the key to start the car, put the car into drive, and press the gas pedal. You don't need to know how everything is wired together in the engine under the vehicle's hood. You probably do not even care. All you care about is that you can drive the car when you perform the behaviors mentioned.

In this section, you will explore the disadvantages of focusing on implementation details in your tests. We will show you examples of tests with implementation details. Finally, you will learn how to shift your focus away from thinking about implementation details when testing.

Problems with implementation detail-focused tests

When you write tests that focus on your code's internal details, you create a scenario that increases the chance you have of refactoring your tests whenever you change those details. For example, if you have a state object property named `value` and you write a test to assert that `state.value === 3`, that test will fail if you change the name of the state property to `currentValue`. Having your test code rely on the state object property's name is a problem because it adds a lot of unnecessary extra maintenance and slows down your workflow.

Another problem is that executing this test case yields a false negative because its functionality did not change; only the state name changed. Your tests should give you confidence that the most valuable pieces of your application related to user behavior function as expected and quickly let you know why this is not the case.

Testing implementation details does not verify application code from the most valuable testers' perspective, that of actual users. For example, if you build an account creation form component and ship it to production, an end user interacting with the form via the UI will care about filling out the form and clicking **Submit**, and will expect the next step to happen. You could test the implementation details of invoking the onChange method or updates to the state object property named usernameVal when the user enters new text.

However, you can reduce risk for users if you test that when a user fills out the form, and they click the **Submit** button, the expected results happen. A user will not directly interact with methods or state objects; therefore, our tests can be more valuable by focusing on how users will interact with the form in the UI.

In another example, using the same component, a software engineer is a user who will add the account creation form to the application code along with the required dependencies. The engineer user cares that the component renders as expected when they attempt to use it. Again, you could test the same implementation details mentioned in the first example.

However, you can gain more confidence that the component will work as expected for users if you test that when an engineer renders the form with the required data, the data is present. Keep in mind that this does not mean you should never test the implementation details of your code. In most scenarios, tests that focus on the user provide more confidence than tests that focus on implementation details.

Next, we will show you an example of testing implementation details to illustrate this further.

Implementation detail-focused test example

Let's look at an example test to illustrate further problems with testing the implementation details of components. The test will assert the details of a `Profile` component created with a class-style React component. The `Profile` component accepts employee information and displays it as a card-style element in the DOM. A user can click a button to hide or show the employee's details on the screen. Here is a screenshot of the component's DOM output:

Steve Williams

Software Engineer III

Hide Details

I love building with React!

Figure 1.7 – Profile component

Let's take a look at the code for the `Profile` component. We create a state object with the `showDetails` property initially set to `true`. Next, we create a `setDetails` method that will update the state value of `showDetails`:

```
import React, { Component } from 'react';


export default class Profile extends Component {
  state = { showDetails: true };
  setDetails = () => {
    this.setState((prevState) => ({ showDetails: !prevState.
      showDetails }));
  };
```

Inside the `render` method, we display the `name` and `title` properties passed into the component:

```
render() {
    return (
        <div className="card" style={{ width: "18rem" }}>
            <img
                className="card-img-top"
                src="http://fakeimg.pl/286x180?font=lobster"
                alt="Card cap"
            />
            <div className="card-body">
                <h5 className="card-title">{this.props.name}</h5>
                <p className="card-subtitle mb-2 text-muted">{this.
                    props.title}</p>
```

Note that the `src` image just has a placeholder image, but ideally would accept a passed-in value such as the `name` and `title` property values.

Lastly, we have a button that invokes the `setDetails` method when clicked. The button's text is set to either `Hide Details` or `Display Details` based on the value of `state.showDetails`. Also, employee details are displayed based on the value of `state.showDetails`:

```
button onClick={this.setDetails} className="btn btn-primary">
            {this.state.showDetails ? "Hide Details" : "Display
                Details"}
        </button>
        {this.state.showDetails ? (
            <p className="card-text details">{this.props.
                details}</p>
        ) : null}
    </div>
    </div>
    );
}
}
```

Now, let's look at the test code for the `Profile` component. The test is created using Enzyme, which is a React testing utility that makes it difficult to avoid testing implementation details and Jest. In the test file, we have one test with four assertions for the `Profile` component.

We mount the `Profile` component into the DOM with values set for the required dependencies. We set the `name` property to `"John Doe"`, the `title` property to `"Team Lead"`, and the `details` property to `"This is my 5th year and I love helping others"`:

```
import React from 'react';
import { mount } from 'enzyme';
import Profile from './Profile';
test('setDetails sets the state value', () => {
  const wrapper = mount(
    <Profile
      name="John Doe"
      title="Team Lead"
      details="This is my 5th year and I love helping others"
    />
  );
```

Next, we make assertions on the resulting DOM output of the `Profile` component. We assert the value of the `showDetails` state property. We search the DOM for an element with the `.card-text.details` class and assert the value of its text. Then, we invoke the component's `setDetails` method:

```
  expect(wrapper.state('showDetails')).toEqual(true);
  expect(wrapper.find('.card-text.details').props().children).
    toEqual(
    'This is my 5th year and I love helping others'
  );
wrapper.instance().setDetails();
```

Finally, we assert that the `showDetails` state property has changed and that the element with the `.card-text.details` class is no longer in the DOM:

```
expect(wrapper.state('showDetails')).toEqual(false);
expect(wrapper.update().find('.card-text.details').exists()).
    toBeFalsy();
});
```

To summarize, the test makes assertions on the following implementation details:

- The state object
- The `setDetails` method
- The element with the class `.card-text.details`

If one of the state object's properties changes, our test will break. If the `setDetails` method's name is changed or replaced with some other code without affecting the functionality, our test will fail. Lastly, if the class name the test uses to select the element changes, our test will break.

As you can see, the test's assertions can yield false negative results if the implementation details change as compared to functionality changes. This increases the likelihood of a need to update the test often, and not test based on actual users' behavior.

Now that you understand the disadvantages of testing implementation details, let's look at better ways to test.

How to move away from implementation detail testing

Now that you understand the disadvantages of implementation detail-focused testing, how do you write tests to ensure that they will work as expected for users? Simply create your tests as if the software under test was a black box. Your thought process should be, *What are the expectations a software engineer or end user may have while using this piece of software?* Let's look at the following `Counter` component with **Add** and **Subtract** buttons, which display the current value. The value is increased or decreased by 1 based on the clicked button:

Figure 1.8 – Counter component

Try to think of as many black-box scenarios a software engineer or end user may perform while using the form.

Here are a few sample scenarios:

- When the `Counter` component is rendered, the counter is displayed in the DOM.
- When a user clicks the **Add** button, the current value is increased by 1.
- When a user clicks the **Subtract** button, the current value is decreased by 1.

These scenarios provide assurance that our application works as expected for users compared to focusing on things such as state changes or method calls.

Now you know how to move away from implementation detail-focused test cases and instead focus on actual users. We have seen numerous examples applying the user-focused test approach from previous sections in this chapter.

Summary

In this chapter, you learned about the DOM Testing Library and how it is designed to help you write user-focused tests. You now understand how the design of the DOM Testing Library can help you gain confidence that your software works as intended for users. You learned how to install Jest and understand that it is a test runner and the tool we will use to test React code. You learned about `jest-dom`. You know how it can add better error messages and descriptive DOM matchers for your test assertions. You can now install and use `jest-dom` in a project that uses Jest. Finally, you have gained an understanding of the disadvantages of implementation detail-focused testing.

In the next chapter, we will learn how to install and start writing tests for React components using React Testing Library.

Questions

1. Install all the tools mentioned in this chapter and write a simple test.
2. Search for examples of tests online that focus on implementation details. Identify all implementation details and create a refactored version of the tests using the DOM Testing Library.
3. Search MDN Web Docs for articles about ARIA roles. Next, practice writing tests using the `getByRole` query to select various elements.

2
Working with React Testing Library

By the end of this chapter, you will know how to add React Testing Library to React projects. React Testing Library is a modern tool for testing the UI output of React components from the perspective of end users. You will learn how to properly structure tests using the methods from the API. You will learn how to test presentational components. Finally, you will learn how to use the debug method to assist in building out your tests.

In this chapter, we're going to cover the following topics:

- Adding React Testing Library to existing projects
- Structuring tests with React Testing Library
- Testing presentational components
- Using the debug method while writing tests

The skills you will learn in this chapter will set the foundation for more complex component scenarios in later chapters.

Technical requirements

For the examples in this chapter, you will need to have Node.js installed on your machine. We will be using the `create-react-app` CLI tool for all code examples. Please familiarize yourself with the tool before starting the chapter if needed. You can find code examples for this chapter here: `https://github.com/PacktPublishing/Simplify-Testing-with-React-Testing-Library/tree/master/Chapter02`.

Adding React Testing Library to existing projects

To get started with React Testing Library, the first thing we need to do is install the tool into our React project. We can either install it manually or use `create-react-app`, a specific React tool that automatically has React Testing Library installed for you.

Manual installation

Add React Testing Library to your project using the following command:

```
npm install --save-dev @testing-library/react
```

Once the tool is installed into your project, you can import the available API methods to use inside your test files.

Next, we will see how to start a React project with React Testing Library when it is already installed for you.

Automatic installation with create-react-app

The `create-react-app` tool allows you to create a one-page React application quickly. The `create-react-app` tool provides a sample application and an associated test to get you started. React Testing Library has become so popular that as of version 3.3.0, the `create-react-app` team added React Testing Library as the default testing tool. The `create-react-app` tool also includes the `user-event` and `jest-dom` utilities. We previously went over `jest-dom` in *Chapter 1, Exploring React Testing Library*. We will cover the `user-event` utility in *Chapter 3, Testing Complex Components with React Testing Library*.

So, if you are using at least version 3.3.0 of `create-react-app`, you get a React application with React Testing Library, `user-event`, and `jest-dom` automatically installed and configured.

There are two ways you can run the `create-react-app` tool to create a new React application. By default, both ways of running the `create-react-app` tool will automatically install the latest version of `create-react-app`. The first way is with `npx`, which allows you to create a React project without needing to have the `create-react-app` tool globally installed on your local machine:

```
npx create-react-app your-project-title-here --use-npm
```

When using the preceding command, be sure to replace `your-project-title-here` with a title to describe your unique project. Also, notice the `--use-npm` flag at the end of the command. By default, when you create a project using `create-react-app`, it uses Yarn as the package manager for the project. We will use `npm` as the package manager throughout this book. We can tell `create-react-app` we want to use `npm` as the package manager instead of Yarn using the `--use-npm` flag.

The second way to create a React application with `create-react-app` is by installing the tool globally to run on your local machine. Use the following command to install the tool globally:

```
npm install -g create-react-app
```

In the previous command, we used the `-g` command to globally install the tool on our machine. Once the tool is installed on your machine, run the following command to create a project:

```
create-react-app your-project-title-here --use-npm
```

Like the command we ran in the previous example to create a project using `npx`, we create a new project titled `your-project-title-here` using `npm` as the package manager.

Now you know how to manually install React Testing Library or have it automatically installed using `create-react-app`. Next, we will learn about common React Testing Library API methods used to structure tests.

Structuring tests with React Testing Library

To structure and write our test code, we will use the *Arrange-Act-Assert* pattern that's typical in writing unit tests. There are a few ways to use React Testing Library API to structure tests, but we will be using React Testing Library team's recommended approach to render React elements into the **Document Object Model (DOM)**, select resulting DOM elements, and make assertions on the expected resulting behavior.

Rendering elements

To test your React components' output, you need a way to render them into the DOM. The React Testing Library's `render` method takes a passed-in component, puts it inside a `div` element, and attaches it to the DOM, as we can see here:

```
import { render} from '@testing-library/react'
import Jumbotron from './Jumbotron'

it('displays the heading, () => {
    render(<Jumbotron />)
}
```

In the previous code, we have a test file. First, we import the `render` method from React Testing Library. Next, we import the Jumbotron component we want to test. Finally, we arrange our test code in the `it` method by using the `render` method to render the component to test.

It is necessary to write additional code to clean up our test in many testing frameworks. For example, if a component is rendered into the DOM for one test, it needs to be removed before the next test is executed. Removing the component from the DOM allows the following test to start from a clean slate and not be affected by code from previous tests. React Testing Library's `render` method makes test cleanup easier by automatically taking care of removing components from the DOM, so there is no need to write additional code to clean up the state affected by previous tests.

Now that you know how to arrange a test by rendering a component into the DOM for testing, we will learn how to interact with the component's resulting DOM output in the next section.

Selecting elements in the component DOM output

Once we have rendered our component to test into the DOM, the next step is to select elements. We will do this by querying the output as a user would. The DOM Testing Library API has a `screen` object that is included with React Testing Library, allowing you to query the DOM:

```
import { render, screen } from '@testing-library/react'
```

In the previous code, we imported `screen` from React Testing Library just like we imported `render`. The `screen` object exposes many methods, such as `getByText` or `getByRole`, used to query the DOM for elements, similar to actual users that we can use in our tests. For example, we might have a component that renders the following DOM output:

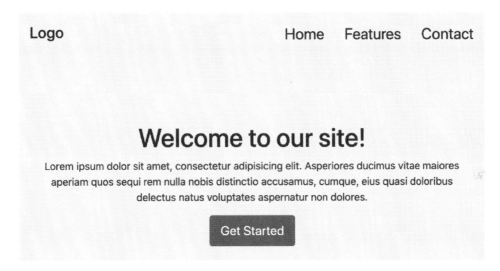

Logo   Home   Features   Contact

Welcome to our site!

Lorem ipsum dolor sit amet, consectetur adipisicing elit. Asperiores ducimus vitae maiores aperiam quos sequi rem nulla nobis distinctio accusamus, cumque, eius quasi doloribus delectus natus voluptates aspernatur non dolores.

Get Started

Figure 2.1 – Jumbotron component

If we wanted to search the DOM for the element with the text **Welcome to our site!**, we could do so in two ways.

One way would be using the `getByText` method:

```
it('displays the heading', () => {
  render(<Jumbotron />)
  screen.getByText(/welcome to our site!/i)
})
```

The `getByText` method will query the DOM, looking for an element with text matching **Welcome to our site!**. Notice how we use a regular expression inside the `getByText` method. A user looking for the element wouldn't care if the text was in upper or lower case, so `getByText` and all other `screen` object methods follow the same approach.

A second way we could query the DOM for the element with the text **Welcome to our site!** is by using the getByRole method:

```
it('displays the heading, () => {
  render(<Jumbotron />)
  screen.getByRole('heading', { name: /welcome to our
    site!/i })
})
```

The getByRole method allows you to query the DOM in ways similar to how anyone, including those using screen readers, would search. A screen reader would look for an element with the role heading and the text welcome to our site!. There are many other methods available on the screen object to query elements based on how you decide to find them. The DOM Testing Library team recommends using the getByRole method to select elements as much as possible in the documentation.

Also, because our test code essentially says, search for a heading element with the text 'welcome to our site!', it is more explicit than the previous example, where we used getByText to search for any element that has the text 'welcome to our site!'.

In the *Enhancing jest assertions with jest-dom* section of *Chapter 1, Exploring React Testing Library*, we learned that the methods of jest-dom provide context-specific error messages.

The methods on the screen object provide the same benefits. For example, if you attempt to use getByRole to select an element that is not present in the DOM, the method will stop test execution and provide the following error message:

```
Unable to find an accessible element with the role
  "heading" and name `/fake/i`
```

In the previous code, the error message explicitly tells you that the query method did not find the element. Also, the error message helps by logging elements that are selectable based on the rendered DOM:

```
heading:
    Name "Logo":
    <h3
        class="navbar-brand mb-0"
        style="font-size: 1.5rem;"
    />
```

```
        Name "Welcome to our site!":
        <h1 />
```

In the preceding code, the logged elements help by providing a visual representation of the DOM to understand better why the element you searched for was not found. Now you know how to select elements using React Testing Library.

We will learn more advanced ways of interacting with components, such as clicking or entering text, in *Chapter 3, Testing Complex Components with React Testing Library*.

Next, we will learn how to assert the expected output of components.

Asserting expected behavior

The last step in the test structure is to make assertions on behavior. In the *Enhancing jest assertions with jest-dom* section of *Chapter 1, Exploring React Testing Library*, we learned how to install and use the jest-dom tool to make assertions. Building on our test where we searched for the heading element with the text welcome to our site!, we can use the toBeInTheDocument method from jest-dom to verify whether the element is in the DOM:

```
it('displays the heading', () => {
  render(<Jumbotron />)

  expect(
    screen.getByRole('heading', { name: /welcome to our
      site!/i })
  ).toBeInTheDocument()
})
```

If the element is not found, we will receive error messages and visual feedback to help determine the source of the problem logged to the console, similar to what we saw in the *Interacting with the component DOM output* section. If we get the expected behavior, then we will receive feedback in the console that our test passed, as shown in the following screenshot:

```
PASS  src/Jumbotron.test.js
  ✓ displays the heading (64ms)

Test Suites: 1 passed, 1 total
Tests:       1 passed, 1 total
Snapshots:   0 total
Time:        1.803s, estimated 2s
```

Figure 2.2 – Jumbotron component test results

In the previous screenshot, the results indicate that the **displays the heading** test passes. Now you know how to make assertions on the output of components with React Testing Library. The skills learned in this section have set the foundational skills needed in the next section, where we start testing presentational components.

Testing presentational components

In this section, we will use our knowledge of installing and structuring tests with React Testing Library to test presentational components. Presentational components are components that do not manage state. Typically, you use presentational components to display data passed down from parent components as props or to display hardcoded data directly in the component itself.

Creating snapshot tests

Snapshot tests are provided by Jest and are great to use when you simply want to make sure the HTML output of a component does not change unexpectedly. Suppose a developer does change the component's HTML structure, for example, by adding another paragraph element with static text. In that case, the snapshot test will fail and provide a visual of the changes so you can respond accordingly. The following is an example of a presentational component that renders hardcoded data related to travel services to the DOM:

```
const Travel = () => {
  return (
    <div className="card text-center m-1" style={{ width:
```

```
        '18rem' }}>
      <i className="material-icons" style={{ fontSize:
        '4rem' }}>
        airplanemode_active
      </i>
      <h4>Travel Anywhere</h4>
```

The component displays an airplane icon in the previous code snippet in an `<i>` element and a heading inside an `<h4>` element:

```
<p className="p-1">
          Our premium package allows you to take exotic trips
          anywhere at the cheapest prices!
      </p>
    </div>
  )
}
export default Travel
```

In the last piece of the component, the preceding code snippet displays text inside a paragraph element. The resulting DOM output looks like the following:

Figure 2.3 – Travel component

Since the component simply displays a few lines of static hardcoded text, it makes it a good candidate for a snapshot test. In the following example, we use snapshot testing to test the `Travel` component:

```
import { render } from '@testing-library/react'
import Travel from './Travel'

it('displays the header and paragraph text', () => {
  const { container } = render(<Travel />)
```

First, in our test file we import the `render` method from React Testing Library. Next, we import the `Travel` component. Then, we use object destructuring to get `container` off the rendered component. `container` represents the resulting HTML output of the component. Finally, we use the `toMatchInlineSnapshot` method from Jest to capture the resulting HTML output.

The following is a portion of the snapshot for the `Travel` component output we saw at the beginning of this section:

```
expect(container).toMatchInlineSnapshot(`
  <div>
    <div
      class="card text-center m-1"
      style="width: 18rem;"
    >
      <i
        class="material-icons"
        style="font-size: 4rem;"
      >
        airplanemode_active
      </i>
```

Now, if in the future a developer changes the output of the `Travel` component, the test will fail and inform us of the unexpected changes. For example, a developer may change the heading from `Travel Anywhere` to `Go Anywhere`:

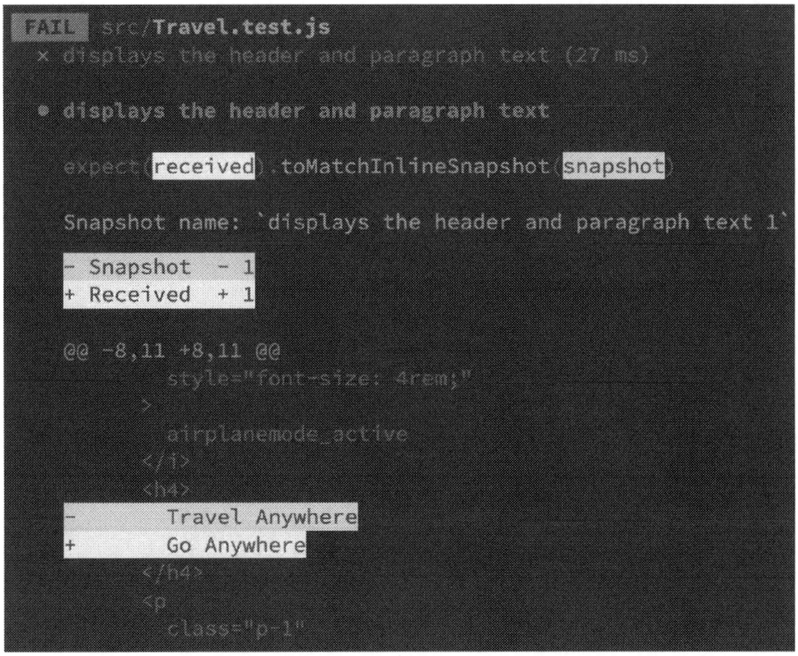

Figure 2.4 – Failed travel snapshot test

The preceding screenshot shows that the test failed and shows us which lines changed. `Travel Anywhere` is the text the snapshot is expected to receive that differed from the received text, **Go Anywhere**. Also, the line number, **8**, and position in the line, **11**, where the difference was found are also pointed out. If the change was intentional, we can update our snapshot with the new change. Run the following command to update the snapshot:

```
npm test -- -u
```

If your tests are currently running in watch mode, simply press the *U* key on your keyboard to update the snapshot. If the change was not intentional, we can simply change the text back to the original value inside the component file.

Now that you know how to create snapshot tests for presentational components, we will now learn how to verify properties passed into presentational components.

Testing expected properties

Presentational components can have data passed into them as props, instead of hardcoded data directly in the component. The following is an example of a presentational component that expects an array of objects for employees to display in a table:

```
const Table = props => {
  return (
    <table className="table table-striped">
      <thead className="thead-dark">
        <tr>
          <th scope="col">Name</th>
          <th scope="col">Department</th>
          <th scope="col">Title</th>
        </tr>
      </thead>
```

In the preceding code snippet, the component has a table with the headings Name, Department, and Title for each employee. The following is the table body:

```
      <tbody>
        {props.employees.map(employee => {
          return (
            <tr key={employee.id}>
              <td>{employee.name}</td>
              <td>{employee.department}</td>
              <td>{employee.title}</td>
            </tr>
          )
        })}
      </tbody>
    </table>
  )
}
export default Table
```

In the preceding code snippet, we iterate over the employees array from the props object inside the table body. We create a table row for each employee, access the employee's name, department, and title, and render the data into a table cell element.

The following is an example of the resulting DOM output:

Name	Department	Title
John Smith	Sales	Senior Sales Agent
Sarah Jenkins	Engineering	Senior Full-Stack Engineer
Tim Reynolds	Design	Designer

Figure 2.5 – Table component

The `Table` component displays rows of employees that match the expected shape of an array of objects with **Name**, **Department**, and **Title** properties. We can test that the component properly accepts and displays the rows of employee data in the DOM:

```
import { render, screen } from '@testing-library/react'
import fakeEmployees from './mocks/employees'
import Table from './Table'

it('renders with expected values', () => {
  render(<Table employees={fakeEmployees} />)
```

First, we import the `render` method and `screen` object from React Testing Library. Next, we pass in a fake array of employee objects called `fakeEmployees`, created for testing purposes, and the `Table` component. The `fakeEmployees` data looks like the following:

```
const fakeEmployees = [
  {
    id: 1,
    name: 'John Smith',
    department: 'Sales',
    title: 'Senior Sales Agent'
  },
  {
    id: 2,
    name: 'Sarah Jenkins',
    department: 'Engineering',
    title: 'Senior Full-Stack Engineer'
  },
```

```
    { id: 3, name: 'Tim Reynolds', department: 'Design',
        title: 'Designer' }
]
```

Finally, we create the main test code to verify the `fakeEmployee` data is present in the DOM:

```
it('renders with expected values', () => {
    render(<Table employees={fakeEmployees} />)
    expect(screen.getByRole('cell', { name: /john smith/i
      })).toBeInTheDocument()
    expect(screen.getByRole('cell', { name: /engineering/i
      })).toBeInTheDocument()
    expect(screen.getByRole('cell', { name: /designer/i
      })).toBeInTheDocument()
})
```

For the preceding code snippet's assertions, we verified that at least one piece of each object was present in the DOM. You could also verify that every piece of data is present in the DOM if that aligns with your testing objectives. Be sure to verify that your code tests what you expect it is testing. For example, try making the test fail by using the `screen` object to query the DOM for employee data that should not be present. If the test fails, you can be more confident that the code tests what you expect.

Although most of the time we want to avoid implementation details and write our tests from the perspective of the user, there may be times where testing specific details is important to our testing goals. For example, if it might be important to you to verify that the striped color theme is present in the rendered version of the table component. The `toHaveAttribute` assertion method of `Jest-dom` can be used in this situation:

```
it('has the correct class', () => {
    render(<Table employees={fakeEmployees} />)
    expect(screen.getByRole('table')).toHaveAttribute(
      'class',
      'table table-striped'
    )
})
```

In the preceding code snippet, we created a test to verify that the table component has the correct class attribute. First, we render the `Table` component with employees. Next, we select the `table` element using the `getByRole` method off the `screen` object. Finally, we assert that the component has a `class` attribute with the value `table table-striped`. By using `toHaveAttribute`, we can assert the value of component attributes when needed.

Now you know how to test presentational components that accept `props` as data.

In the next section, we will learn how to use the `debug` method to analyze the current state of component output as we build out our tests.

Using the debug method

The `debug` method, accessible from the `screen` object, is a helpful tool in React Testing Library's API that allows you to see the current HTML output of components as you build out your tests. In this section, we will learn how to display the resulting DOM output of an entire component or specific elements.

Debugging the entire component DOM

You can use the `debug` method to log the entire DOM output of a component when you run your test:

```
it('displays the header and paragraph text', () => {
    render(<Travel />)
    screen.debug()
})
```

In the preceding code, we first rendered the `Travel` component into the DOM. Next, we invoked the `debug` method. When we run our test, the following will be logged to the console:

```
PASS  src/Travel.test.js
  ● Console

    console.log
      <body>
        <div>
          <div
            class="card text-center m-1"
            style="width: 18rem;"
          >
            <i
              class="material-icons"
              style="font-size: 4rem;"
            >
              airplanemode_active
            </i>
            <h4>
              Travel Anywhere
            </h4>
            <p
              class="p-1"
            >
              Our premium package allows you to take exotic trips anywhere at the cheapest prices!
            </p>
          </div>
        </div>
      </body>
```

Figure 2.6 – Travel DOM debug

In the previous screenshot, the entire DOM output of the `Travel` component is logged to the screen. Logging the whole output can help you build out your test, especially when interacting with one element in the DOM affects elements elsewhere in the current DOM. Now you know how to log the output of the entire component DOM to the screen. Next, we will learn how to log specific elements of the DOM to the screen.

Debugging specific component elements

You can use the `debug` method to log specific elements of the resulting component DOM to the screen:

```
it('displays the header and paragraph text', () => {
  render(<Travel />)
  const header = screen.getByRole('heading', { name:
    /travel anywhere/i })

  screen.debug(header)
})
```

In the previous code, first, we rendered the `Travel` component into the DOM. Next, we used the `getByRole` method to query the DOM for a heading with the name `travel anywhere` and saved it to a variable named `header`. Next, we invoked the `debug` method and passed in the `header` variable to the method. When we run our test, the following will be logged to the console:

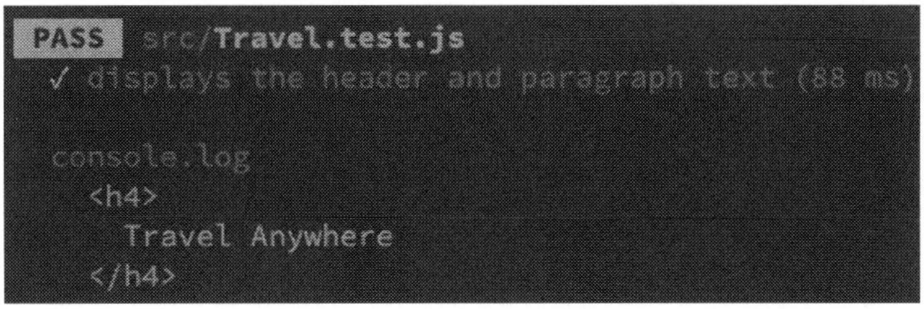

Figure 2.7 – Travel element debug

When you pass in a specific DOM node found by using one of the available query methods, the `debug` method only logs the HTML for the particular node. Logging the output for single elements can help you only focus on specific parts of the component. Be sure to remove any `debug` method code from your tests before making commits because you only need it while building out the test.

Now you know how to use the `debug` method to render the resulting DOM output of your components. The `debug` method is a great visual tool to have while writing new tests and also when troubleshooting failing tests.

Summary

In this chapter, you have learned how to install React Testing Library into your React projects. You now understand how to use the API methods to structure your tests. You know how to test presentational components, which serves as foundational knowledge to build on in the following chapters. Finally, you learned how to debug the HTML output of components as you build out your tests.

In the next chapter, we will learn how to test code with more complexity. We will also learn how to use the **Test-Driven Development** (**TDD**) approach to drive test creation.

Questions

1. What method is used to place React components into the DOM?

2. Name the object that has methods attached to query the DOM for elements.

3. What types of components are good candidates for snapshot tests?

4. What method is used for logging the DOM output of components?

5. Create and test a presentational component that accepts an array of objects as props.

3

Testing Complex Components with React Testing Library

In *Chapter 2, Working with React Testing Library*, we learned how to test presentational components. However, most features are designed to allow user actions that result in changes to the state and resulting output. Testing as many user action scenarios as possible is essential for reducing risk before sending code to production for end users. By the end of this chapter, you will learn how to simulate user actions with the `fireEvent` and `user-event` modules. You will learn how to test components that interact with web service APIs. Finally, you will learn how to use test-driven development as a workflow for building your features.

In this chapter, we're going to cover the following topics:

- Performing actions on components with the `fireEvent` module

- Simulating **Document Object Model (DOM)** events with the `user-event` module

- Testing components that interact with APIs

- Implementing test-driven development with React Testing Library

The skills you gain in this chapter will provide you with a solid understanding of testing the outcomes of user behaviors. You will also gain a different approach to building components from start to finish.

Technical requirements

For the examples in this chapter, you will need to have Node.js installed on your machine. We will be using the `create-react-app` CLI tool for all code examples. Please familiarize yourself with the tool before starting the chapter if needed. Although not a requirement, it may help if you review the material from the previous two chapters before beginning this chapter.

You can find code examples for this chapter here: `https://github.com/PacktPublishing/Simplify-Testing-with-React-Testing-Library/tree/master/Chapter03`.

Testing user events

In this section, we will learn how to simulate user events and test the resulting output. To test component interactions, similar to the case with users, we need methods to simulate DOM events in our tests. Numerous events caused by users can occur on the DOM. For example, a user can perform a keypress event by entering text into an input box, a click event by clicking a button, or they can view drop-down menu items with a mouseover event. The DOM Testing Library provides two libraries to simulate user actions, `fireEvent` and `user-event`, which we are going to see in the following sections.

Simulating user actions with fireEvent

We can use the `fireEvent` module to simulate user actions on the resulting DOM output of components. For example, we can build a reusable `Vote` component that renders the following DOM output:

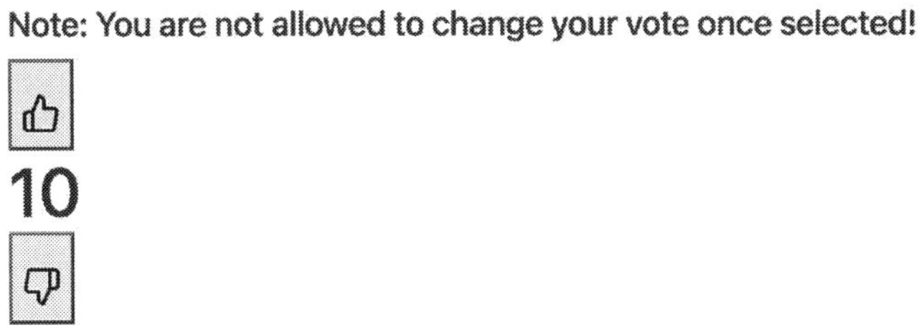

Note: You are not allowed to change your vote once selected!

10

Figure 3.1 – Vote component

In the preceding screenshot, the number **10** represents the likes rating. We have two buttons that a user can click to place a vote and change the likes rating: a thumbs-up button and a thumbs-down button. There is also a disclaimer letting the user know that they are only allowed to vote once. When a user clicks the thumbs-up button, they will see the following output:

Note: You are not allowed to change your vote once selected!

11

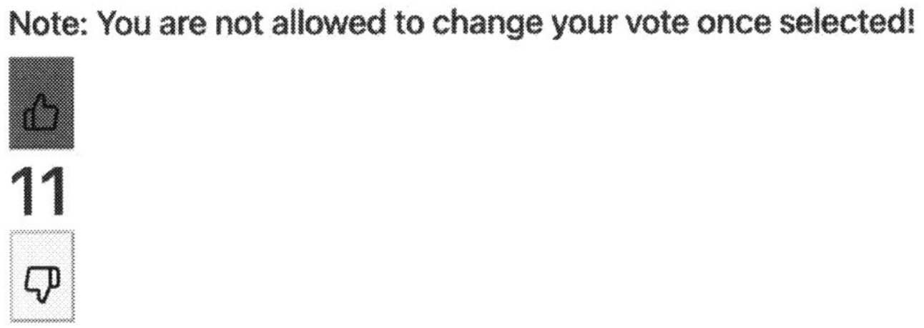

Figure 3.2 – Thumbs-up vote

In the previous screenshot, the likes rating increased from **10** to **11**. When a user clicks the thumbs-down button, they will see the following output:

Note: You are not allowed to change your vote once selected!

9

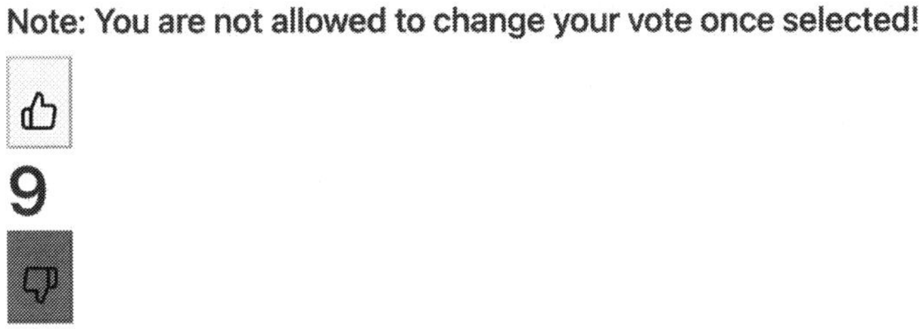

Figure 3.3 – Thumbs-down vote

In the previous screenshot, the likes rating has decreased from **10** to **9**. The act of clicking the button is an event we can simulate with `fireEvent`. In the code implementation for the `Vote` component, an event handler is called inside the component with logic to update the likes we see on the screen:

```
const handleLikeVote = () => dispatch({ type: 'LIKE' })
const handleDislikeVote = () => dispatch({ type:
  'DISLIKE' })


return (
  <div className="h1">
    <h5>Note: You are not allowed to change your vote
      once selected!</h5>
    <button
      onClick={handleLikeVote}
      disabled={hasVoted}
      style={clickedLike ? { background: 'green' } :
        null}
    >
      <img src={thumbsUp} alt="thumbs up" />
    </button>
```

In the preceding code block, the button has an `onClick` event handler attached. When the like button is clicked, the event handler calls the `handleLikeVote` method, which calls another method, `dispatch`, which updates the likes rating.

> **Important Note**
>
> Please refer to the *Chapter 3, Testing Complex Components with React Testing Library*, code samples, found in the *Technical requirements* section, to see the component in its entirety.

We can write a test to assert the output of making a vote:

```
import { fireEvent, render, screen } from '@testing-library/
react'
import Vote from './Vote'


test('increases total likes by one', () => {
  render(<Vote totalGlobalLikes={10} />)
```

In the preceding code block, we import the `fireEvent`, `render`, and `screen` methods from React Testing Library. Next, we import the `Vote` component to test. Then, we arrange our test code in the `test` method and use the `render` method to render the `Vote` component with the value `10` for the `totalGlobalLikes` property passed in to the component.

The `totalGlobalLikes` property is the number we initially see on the screen when the component is rendered and represents the application-wide state for the likes. In a fully completed application, we would pass the `totalGlobalLikes` value down to the `Vote` component via a parent component. Next, we will interact with and assert the output of the rendered component:

```
expect(screen.getByText(/10/i)).toBeInTheDocument()
  fireEvent.click(screen.getByRole('button', { name:
    /thumbs up/i }))
  expect(screen.getByText(11).toBeInTheDocument()
  expect(screen.getByRole('button', { name: /thumbs up/i
    })).toHaveStyle(
    'background: green'
  )
})
```

In the preceding code block, first, we assert that the `Vote` component's local version of `totalGlobalLikes` is in the document with a value equal to `10`. Next, we use the `click` method of `fireEvent` to click the button with the name `thumbs up`. Next, we assert that the value of `totalGlobalLikes` updates in the document to `11`. Finally, we assert that the `thumbs up` button's background color has changed to `green`.

In many cases, using `fireEvent` is completely fine. However, it does have some limitations. For example, when a user performs an action such as entering text into an input box, many events occur, such as `keydown` and `keyup`. Now, `fireEvent` has methods to achieve these individual actions, but it doesn't have one way to handle them all together in sequence.

Next, we will learn about using the `user-event` library to address the `fireEvent` module's limitations.

Simulating user actions with user-event

The user-event library is an enhanced version of fireEvent. In the previous section, we learned that fireEvent has methods to simulate various events that occur when a user enters text into an input box. The user-event library has many methods, such as click or type, that automatically simulate all the events that occur when a user performs actions on the DOM. The advantage is that user-event methods provide more value compared to fireEvent methods.

create-react-app comes with user-event already installed. For projects not using create-react-app, use the following command to install:

```
npm install --save-dev @testing-library/user-event
```

We can update the previous section's Vote component test with user-event:

```
import { render, screen } from '@testing-library/react'
import user from '@testing-library/user-event'
import Vote from './Vote'


test('increases total likes by one', () => {
  render(<Vote totalGlobalLikes={10} />)
  expect(screen.getByText(/10/i)).toBeInTheDocument()
  user.click(screen.getByRole('button', { name: /thumbs
    up/i }))
  expect(screen.getByText(/11/i)).toBeInTheDocument()
  expect(screen.getByRole('button', { name: /thumbs up/i
    })).toHaveStyle(
    'background: green'
  )
})
```

In the previous code, we imported the user-event library as user. Finally, we used the click method of user-event to click the thumbs up button. Our test provides more value because we are more closely simulating user DOM actions. The React Testing Library team recommends using user-event as much as possible, so we will not use fireEvent in any more examples throughout the remainder of this book.

When we introduced the `Vote` component in the previous section, we mentioned that a user could only vote once. We can write a test to handle that scenario:

```
test('A user can only vote once', () => {
  render(<Vote totalGlobalLikes={10} />)
  const thumbsUpBtn = screen.getByRole('button', { name:
    /thumbs up/i })
  const thumbsDownBtn = screen.getByRole('button', { name:
    /thumbs down/i })

  expect(screen.getByText(/10/i)).toBeInTheDocument()
  user.click(thumbsUpBtn)
  user.click(thumbsUpBtn)
  expect(screen.getByText(/11/i)).toBeInTheDocument()

  user.click(thumbsDownBtn)
  expect(screen.getByText(/11/i)).toBeInTheDocument()
})
```

In the preceding code, first, we grab the `thumbs up` and `thumbs down` buttons. Then, we verify the current total likes is `10` and click the `thumbs up` button twice. Next, we verify the total likes is `11`. Finally, we click the `thumbs down` button and assert that the total likes count is still `11`. As another test case, we can also verify that the local version of `totalGlobalLikes` decreases by one when a user clicks the `thumbs down` button:

```
test('decreases total likes by one', () => {
  render(<Vote totalGlobalLikes={10} />)

  expect(screen.getByText(/10/i)).toBeInTheDocument()
  user.click(screen.getByRole('button', { name: /thumbs
    down/i }))
  expect(screen.getByText(/9/i)).toBeInTheDocument()

  expect(screen.getByRole('button', { name: /thumbs down/i
    })).toHaveStyle(
    'background: red'
  )
})
```

We click the `thumbs down` button and verify the total likes decreased from `10` to `9`, and the background color changed to `red` in the preceding code.

When we run all the tests for the `Vote` component, we get the following results indicating all tests passed:

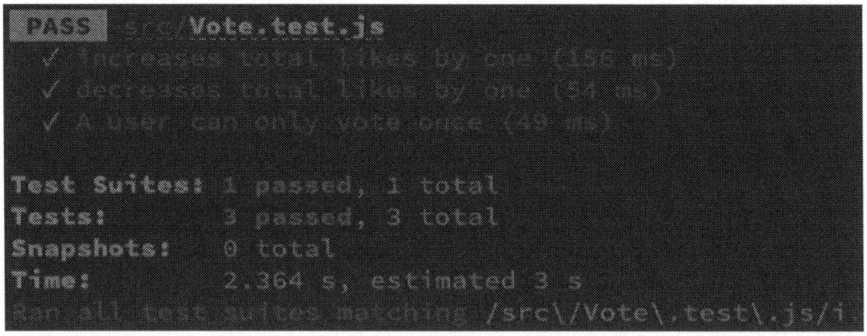

```
PASS  src/Vote.test.js
  ✓ increases total likes by one (156 ms)
  ✓ decreases total likes by one (54 ms)
  ✓ A user can only vote once (49 ms)

Test Suites: 1 passed, 1 total
Tests:       3 passed, 3 total
Snapshots:   0 total
Time:        2.364 s, estimated 3 s
Ran all test suites matching /src\/Vote\.test\.js/i
```

Figure 3.4 – Vote component test results

The preceding screenshot shows that the **increases total likes by one, decreases total likes by one**, and **A user can only vote once** tests have passed in the `Vote.test.js` file.

In another example, we might create an input component for employees that accepts their name:

Figure 3.5 – Employee email input

When the employee enters their name, the component appends it to the company's website name and displays the result to the screen:

Figure 3.6 – Completed employee email input

If the employee enters a first and last name separated by a space, the name is concatenated with a `.`:

| jane doe | @software-plus.com |

jane.doe@software-plus.com

Figure 3.7 – Concatenated employee email input

We can use the `type` method of `user-event` to simulate typing into the employee email component and make an assertion on the result as follows:

```
import { render, screen } from '@testing-library/react'
import user from '@testing-library/user-event'
import EmployeeEmail from './EmployeeEmail'

test('it accepts a username and displays to the screen', ()
  => {
  render(<EmployeeEmail />)
  const input = screen.getByRole('textbox', { name: /enter
    your name/i })

  user.type(input, 'jane doe')

  expect(screen.getByText(/jane.doe@software-
    plus.com/i)).toBeInTheDocument()
})
```

We import the `render`, `screen`, and `user-event` modules in the previous code. Then, we import the `EmployeeEmail` component. We render the component on the screen. Then, we grab the input element and store it in the variable input. Next, we use the `type` method from `user-event` to enter `jane doe` into the input. Finally, we assert that the text `jane.doe@software-plus.com` is in the DOM.

When we run our test, we get the following output indicating the scenario passes as expected:

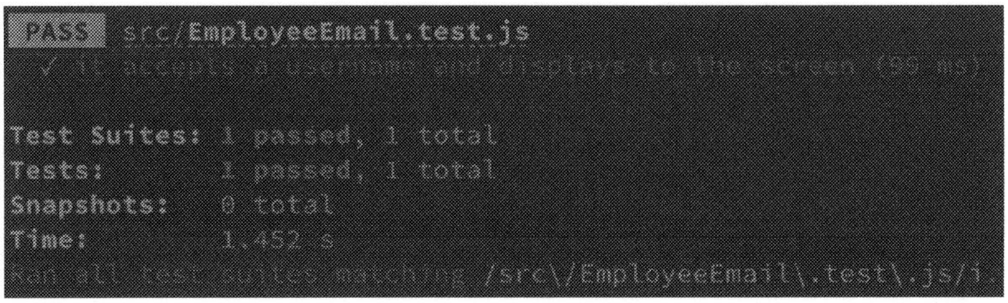

```
PASS  src/EmployeeEmail.test.js
  √ it accepts a username and displays to the screen (99 ms)

Test Suites: 1 passed, 1 total
Tests:       1 passed, 1 total
Snapshots:   0 total
Time:        1.452 s
Ran all test suites matching /src\/EmployeeEmail\.test\.js/i.
```

Figure 3.8 – Employee component test results

The previous screenshot shows that the **it accepts a username and displays to the screen** test passed in the `EmployeeEmail.test.js` file. Now you know how to simulate user actions using the `user-event` module. The skills learned in this section are essential because most of our tests typically will need to involve some type of user action.

Next, we will learn how to test components that call event handlers in isolation.

Testing components that call event handlers in isolation

It is very common to create child components that invoke methods passed down to them from parent components. In the previous section, we had a `Vote` component that included two buttons in the same component, which can be seen in the following code block:

```
<button
    onClick={voteLike}
    disabled={hasVoted}
    style={clickedLike ? { background: 'green' } :
        null}
>
    <img src={thumbsUp} alt="thumbs up" />
</button>
<div>{totalLikes}</div>
<button
    onClick={voteDislike}
    disabled={hasVoted}
    style={clickedDislike ? { background: 'red' } :
        null}
>
    <img src={thumbsDown} alt="thumbs down" />
</button>
```

We could decide to extract the button code into its own file to become a reusable component:

```
const VoteBtn = props => {
  return (
    <button onClick={props.handleVote}
```

```
        disabled={props.hasVoted}>
        <img src={props.imgSrc} alt={props.altText} />
      </button>
    )
  }
```

In the preceding code block, we have a `VoteBtn` component that accepts `handleVote`, `hasVoted`, `imgSrc`, and `altText` properties passed to the `props` object. The parent component would pass down the props. For this section's purposes, our primary focus is the `handleVote` property. The `handleVote` method is called when a `click` event fires due to clicking the button. When this method runs inside the `Vote` component, the result is updating the local version of `totalGlobalLikes`. The resulting screen output of the button is as follows:

Figure 3.9 – Vote button

In the preceding screenshot, we see a `Vote` component with a `thumbs up` image. To test the `VoteBtn` component in isolation, we need to provide properties to the component since it's no longer wrapped in a component that provides them automatically. Jest provides functions that serve as test doubles to replace the real versions of methods inside our tests.

A test double is a generic term used to represent an object that replaces a real object for testing purposes. Test doubles used as placeholders for dependencies such as an API or database are known as **stubs**. However, when a test double is used to make assertions against, it is known as a **mock**. For example, we can use the `jest.fn` function to replace `handleVote` inside our test:

```
import { render, screen } from '@testing-library/react'
import user from '@testing-library/user-event'
import thumbsUp from './images/thumbs-up.svg'
import VoteBtn from './VoteBtn'

test('invokes handleVote', () => {
  const mockHandleVote = jest.fn()
  render(
```

```
<VoteBtn
    handleVote={mockHandleVote}
    hasVoted={false}
    imgSrc={thumbsUp}
    altText="vote like"
/>
)
```

In the preceding code block, first, we import the `render` and `screen` methods from React Testing Library. Next, we import the `user-event` module. Then, we import the `thumbsUp` image and the `VoteBtn` component we want to test. Then, inside the `test` method, we create a `jest` function to use as a mock and assign it to the `mockHandleVote` variable.

Next, we render the `VoteBtn` component into the DOM and pass `mockHandleVote` and other properties to the component. Now that our test code is arranged, we can perform actions and make assertions:

```
user.click(screen.getByRole('button', { name: /vote
    like/i }))


expect(mockHandleVote).toHaveBeenCalled()
expect(mockHandleVote).toHaveBeenCalledTimes(1)
})
```

In the previous code, we click the button with the name **vote like**. Finally, we make two assertions. The first assertion verifies the `mockHandleVote` method is called when a user clicked the button. The second assertion confirms the `mockHandleVote` method was called exactly one time. The `mockHandleVote` assertions can be important when you need to be sure the function is used correctly. When we run our test, we get the following output indicating the scenario passes as expected:

```
PASS  src/VoteBtn.test.js
  ✓ invokes handleVote (83 ms)

Test Suites: 1 passed, 1 total
Tests:       1 passed, 1 total
Snapshots:   0 total
Time:        1.207 s
Ran all test suites matching /src\/VoteBtn\.test\.js/i.
```

Figure 3.10 – Vote button component test results

The previous screenshot shows that the **invokes handleVote** test passed in the `VoteBtn.test.js` file. It should be noted that although we were able to verify that the event handler is called, we are not able to confirm whether the button state changes to disabled after being clicked. We would need to include the parent component and write an integration test to verify that behavior. We will learn how to approach these scenarios in *Chapter 4, Integration Testing and Third-Party Libraries in Your Application*.

Now you know how to test event handlers in isolated components with test doubles. In this section, we learned how to simulate and test user interactions. We learned how to mimic actions with `fireEvent` and `user-event`. We also learned how to use test doubles to test event handlers. The skills learned in this section will help you in the next section when we learn how to test components that interact with APIs.

Testing components that interact with APIs

This section will build on our knowledge of testing event handlers from the previous section by looking at how to test components that send and receive data from APIs. In our component unit tests, we can reduce application risk with our testing efforts by using tools that act as test doubles in place of real APIs. Using test doubles in place of the actual API, we can avoid slow internet connections or receive dynamic data resulting in unpredictable test results.

We will learn how to install and use **Mock Service Worker** (**MSW**) as a test double in tests to capture API requests initiated by our components and return mock data. We will test a component designed for users to search for drinks data from an API. We will also learn how to use MSW as a development server. The concepts in this section will help us understand how to verify communication between the frontend and API servers.

Requesting API data with fetch

We can create a component that allows a user to search for drinks from TheCockTailDB (`https://www.thecocktaildb.com`), a free open source service that will play the backend API's role. Our component will access the service and request data. When the component first renders, the user sees an input field and a **Search** button:

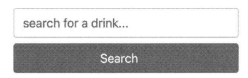

Figure 3.11 – Drink search component

When a user searches for drinks, the API returns drink data similar to the following:

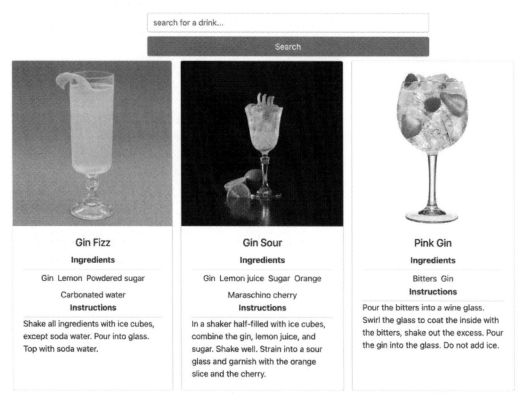

Figure 3.12 – Drink search results

In the preceding screenshot, a user searched for `gin` and received an array of results from the API. If a user searches for drinks that don't return results, a **No drinks found** message is displayed on the screen:

Figure 3.13 – No drink search results

If a user attempts a search and the API server is inaccessible, a **Service unavailable** message is displayed:

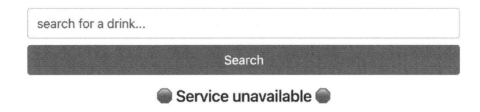

Figure 3.14 – Drink search request error

Our component will use an HTTP request module designed to request drink data from the API using the fetch method, a tool included in browsers to make HTTP requests:

```
const fetchDrinks = async drinkQuery => {
  const response = await fetch(
    `https://www.thecocktaildb.com/api/json/v1/1/search.php?s=$
{drinkQuery}`
  )

  const data = await response.json()
  return data.drinks
}
export default fetchDrinks
```

In the preceding code block, fetchDrinks accepts a drinkQuery parameter representing the search data and makes an API request to return drinks data.

The Drink Search component has a form that, when submitted, will call the handleDrinkQuery method, which ultimately invokes the request module with the drinks to search:

```
<form onSubmit={handleDrinkQuery}>
  <input
    placeholder='search for a drink...'
    type='search'
    value={drinkQuery}
    onChange={(event) => setDrinkQuery(event.target.value)}
  />
  <button type='submit'>Search</button>
</form>
```

When the `request` module sends a response that includes an array of drinks, the `Drink Search` component will call `drinkResults`, a method that renders `drinks` on the screen:

```
{drinks && <div>{drinkResults()}</div>}
```

If the response does not return any drinks, then the `No drinks found` code is rendered:

```
{!drinks && <h5> No drinks found </h5>}
```

If there is an error communicating with the server, then the `Service unavailable` code is rendered:

```
{error && <h5>◉ Service unavailable ◉</h5>}
```

Now we understand how the `Drink Search` component behaves based on user interactions. Next, we will learn how to create mock API data to test the component.

Creating mock API data with MSW

MSW is a tool we can use to capture API requests initiated by our components and return mocked responses. When our frontend React application makes an HTTP request to an API server, MSW will intercept the request before it reaches the network and respond with mock data. Use the following command to install MSW into your project:

```
npm install msw --save-dev
```

To get started using MSW, first, we will create a mock response route handler to override matching calls to specific URLs by our component:

```
import { rest } from 'msw'

export const handlers = [
  rest.get(
    'https://www.thecocktaildb.com/api/json/v1/1/search.php',
    (req, res, ctx) => {
      return res(
        ctx.status(200),
        ctx.json({
          drinks: [
            {
```

```
        idDrink: 1,
        strDrinkThumb: './images/thumbs-down.svg',
        strDrink: 'test drink',
        strInstructions: 'test instructions',
        strIngredient1: 'test ingredient'
    }
  ]
```

In the preceding code block, we imported `rest` from `msw`. The `rest` object allows us to specify the `request` type to `mock`. Inside the `get` method, we specify the route we will override when a *GET* request is made. In the `callback` parameter of the `get` method, three parameters are accepted –the `req` parameter provides information about the request, such as the data sent in the request. The `res` parameter is a function used to make the mocked response. The `ctx` parameter provides a context for the response functions to send.

Inside `ctx`, we create a `200` response status code indicating a successful request, and lastly, we create JSON data to return, which will be an array of drinks. You may notice that the *GET* request route does not match the entire URL used in the HTTP request module from the previous section. MSW will pattern match URLs, making the need to use the exact URL string unnecessary.

Next, we will create our mock server and pass in the mock response route handler:

```
import { setupServer } from 'msw/node'
import { handlers } from './handlers'
export const mockServer = setupServer(...handlers)
```

In the previous code, first, we import `setupServer` from `msw/node`, which will be used to intercept requests made to the route handler created in the previous code snippet. We use `msw/node` because our test code will run in a Node.js environment. Next, we import the route handlers. Finally, we pass the handlers to `setupServer` and export the code via the `mockServer` variable. Now that we have our server set up, we can write a test for the `DrinkSearch` component.

Testing the DrinkSearch component

To get started testing the component, first, we will import the required code and start our mock server:

```
import { render, screen} from '@testing-library/react'
import user from '@testing-library/user-event'
import DrinkSearch from './DrinkSearch'
import { mockServer } from './mocks/server.js'
```

In the preceding code block, first, we import render and screen from React Testing Library. Next, we import the user-event module. Then we import the DrinkSearch component we want to test. Finally, we import mockServer, our mock server. Next, we need to start our mock server and set it up to perform specific actions at different points in the test life cycle:

```
beforeAll(() => mockServer.listen())
afterEach(() => mockServer.resetHandlers())
afterAll(() => mockServer.close())
```

In the preceding code block, first, we set up our mock server to listen to HTTP requests before running any of our tests. Next, we make our mock server reset after each test, so no tests are affected by previous tests. Finally, we shut down our mock server after all tests are finished running. Next, we will create the main test code:

```
test('renders mock drink data, async () => {
  render(<DrinkSearch />)
  const searchInput = screen.getByRole('searchbox')

  user.type(searchInput, 'vodka, {enter}')
```

In the preceding code block, we render the DrinkSearch component. Next, we grab the search input and enter vodka as the drink to search. That {enter} after vodka simulates pressing the *Enter* key on a keyboard. Next, we will make assertions on the outcomes of user actions:

```
  expect(
    await screen.findByRole('img', { name: /test drink/i })
  ).toBeInTheDocument()
  expect(
    screen.getByRole('heading', { name: /test drink/i })
```

```
    ).toBeInTheDocument()
    expect(screen.getByText(/test
      ingredient/i)).toBeInTheDocument()
    expect(screen.getByText(/test
      instructions/i)).toBeInTheDocument()
  })
```

In the preceding code, we use the `findByRole` query method to grab the image element. In previous examples, we solely used `getBy*` queries. The `getBy*` queries can be used in most situations when you expect elements to be available in the current state of the DOM. However, in the previous code, we use a `findBy*` query because the process of communicating with the API is asynchronous, so we need to give our application time to receive a response and update the DOM before attempting to grab an element.

When a `getBy*` query is used to select elements, an error is thrown, and our test fails if the element is not found in the current DOM:

Figure 3.15 – No drink search failing test results

The preceding screenshot shows that the **renders mock drink data** test failed in the `DrinkSearch.test.js` file. The test result output also provides more context for the failure by letting us know it couldn't find an image element with the name `test drink`. The `findBy*` queries will also throw an error when elements are not found, but only after a few seconds, allowing time for the element to appear on the screen.

We can also write a test to verify the output when no results are returned from the API server for our drink search. We can modify the response of our MSW server to set up the scenario:

```
test('renders no drink results', async () => {
  mockServer.use(
    rest.get(
      'https://www.thecocktaildb.com/api/json/v1/1/search.php',
      (req, res, ctx) => {
        return res(
          ctx.status(200),
```

```
            ctx.json({
                drinks: null
            })
        )
    }
    )
)
```

In the preceding code block, we use the use method to override our default mock values to return null. As mentioned in the *Requesting API data with fetch* section, our component will return the No drinks found message when the server does not return an array of drinks. Now that we have our test set up to send the right data, we can write the main test code:

```
    render(<DrinkSearch />)
    const searchInput = screen.getByRole('searchbox')

    user.type(searchInput, 'vodka, {enter}')

    expect(
        await screen.findByRole('heading', { name: / no
            drinks found /i })
    ).toBeInTheDocument()
})
```

We render the DrinkSearch component and search for vodka as in the last test in the preceding code. However, instead of expecting an array of drinks, we expect to see the No drinks found message.

For our next test, we will verify the output when the API server is unavailable. Like we did in the previous test, we will modify the response of our MSW server to set up the test scenario:

```
test('renders service unavailable', async () => {
    mockServer.use(
        rest.get(
            'https://www.thecocktaildb.com/api/json/v1/1/search.php',
            (req, res, ctx) => {
                return res(ctx.status(503))
```

```
        }
    )
)
```

We override our default mock values in the previous code to respond with a `503` status code indicating the API is not available. As mentioned in the *Requesting API data with fetch* section, our component will return the `Service unavailable` message when the server is offline. Now that we have our test set up to send the right response, we can write the main test code:

```
render(<DrinkSearch />)
const searchInput = screen.getByRole('searchbox');

user.type(searchInput, 'vodka, {enter}');

expect(
    await screen.findByRole('heading', { name: /Service
        unavailable/i })
).toBeInTheDocument()
```

Like code in the previous test, we render the `DrinkSearch` component and search for vodka as in the last test. However, now we expect `Service unavailable` to be in the document due to the server sending the `503` error code.

The last test we write will verify that no request is made when a user attempts to submit a blank search query:

```
test('prevents GET request when search input empty', async
    () => {
    render(<DrinkSearch />)
    const searchInput = screen.getByRole('searchbox')

    user.type(searchInput, '{enter}')

    expect(screen.queryByRole('heading')).not.toBeInTheDocument()
})
```

In the previous code, we press the *Enter* key without typing in a search string. When the application first loads, we only see the input field and the button used to search. The application is designed to display additional content that includes heading elements when a search query is submitted to the API. We expect no element with the role of `heading` on the screen using a `queryBy*` query. The `queryBy*` query is preferred when you want to verify that specific elements are not on the screen.

Unlike the `getBy*` and `findBy*` queries, `queryBy*` queries do not throw an error and fail the test when an element is not found. `queryBy*` queries return `null` when an element is not found, allowing you to assert the expected absence of elements in the DOM without test failure. When we run our tests, we should receive the following output indicating our test suite passed:

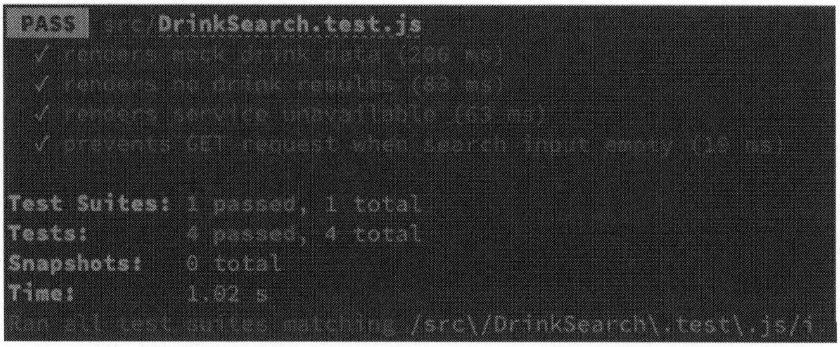

Figure 3.16 – No drink search passing test results

The preceding screenshot shows that the **renders mock drink data**, **renders no drink results**, **renders service unavailable**, and **prevents GET request when search input empty** tests all passed in the `DrinkSearch.test.js` file. Now you know how to create a mock server with MSW to test components that request API data.

Next, we will learn how to use MSW in development.

Using MSW in development

In addition to using MSW to mock HTTP responses in our tests, we can also create mock responses in development. The benefit of having a mock development server is building and testing the frontend even if the backend API is not complete. We need to know what the communication and data exchange will look like between the frontend and backend API to create the right mock responses.

First, we need to add the service worker file to intercept HTTP requests made by our frontend and respond with mock data. The MSW documentation states we should install the file in the public directory of your project. Run the following command from the root of your project to install:

```
npx msw init public/
```

The previous command automatically downloads the service worker file to the public folder. If you are using create-react-app to build your project, the public directory is located at the project's root. We do not need to do anything extra in the file once it's downloaded. Next, we need to create a file in the src/mocks/ directory to set up and start the service worker, similar to what we did in the *Creating mock API data with MSW* section in this chapter.

However, for the mock development server, we will make slight changes to how we set up the server:

```
import { rest, setupWorker } from 'msw'

const drinks = [
  {
    idDrink: '11457',
    strDrink: 'Gin Fizz',
    strInstructions:
      'Shake all ingredients with ice cubes, except soda
        water. Pour into glass. Top with soda water.',
    strDrinkThumb:
          'https://www.thecocktaildb.com/images/media/drink/
            drtihp1606768397.jpg',
    strIngredient1: 'Gin',
    strIngredient2: 'Lemon',
    strIngredient3: 'Powdered sugar',
    strIngredient4: 'Carbonated water'
  },

]
```

In the preceding code, we import `rest` and `setupWorker` from msw. In the *Creating mock API data with MSW* section in this chapter, we imported modules from `msw/node` because our tests run in a Node.js environment. The mock development server will run in the browser, so we do not need to import the Node.js version. Next, we create a `drinks` array of drink data. Then, we set up the routes and responses for the server:

```
export const worker = setupWorker(
  rest.get(
    'https://www.thecocktaildb.com/api/json/v1/1/search.php',
    (req, res, ctx) => {
      return res(
        ctx.status(200),
        ctx.json({
          drinks
        })
      )
    }
  )
)
```

We create a route handler in the preceding code to handle *GET* requests made to the URL attempting to access the cocktail API. We pass in the array of drinks as the response data. In the *Creating mock API data with MSW* section in this chapter, we split the server setup code and route handlers into separate files. We will keep all the server setup code in the same file for the mock development server to achieve the same result. The last thing we need to do is set up our application to run the mock server in the development environment:

```
if (process.env.NODE_ENV === 'development') {
  const { worker } = require('./mocks/browser')
  worker.start()
}

ReactDOM.render(
  <React.StrictMode>
    <App />
  </React.StrictMode>,
  document.getElementById('root')
)
```

In the preceding code, we set up the server to start when the NODE_ENV environment variable is set to development before rendering the App component into the DOM. Applications built with create-react-app already set NODE_ENV to development, so all we need to do is start the application with the npm start script, typical when building create-react-app applications.

Now you know how to create a mock server with MSW to test components that request API data. You also made an MSW server to respond with fake responses in development. Furthermore, you now know when to use the findBy* and queryBy* queries in addition to getBy* queries.

In this section, we learned how to install and use MSW. We tested a component used for searching drinks data from an API. Finally, we learned how to use MSW as a development server. Next, we will learn how to use the test-driven development approach to writing tests.

Implementing test-driven development

Test-Driven Development (**TDD**) entails writing unit tests first and then building the code to pass. The TDD approach allows you to think about whether the code is correct for the tests you want to write. The process provides a perspective that focuses on the least amount of code needed to make tests pass. TDD is also known as **Red, Green, Refactor**. *Red* represents failing tests, *Green* represents passing tests, and as the name says, *Refactor* means refactoring the code while maintaining passing tests. A typical TDD workflow would be the following:

1. Write a test.
2. Run the test, expecting it to fail.
3. Write the minimum amount of code to make the test pass.
4. Rerun the test to verify it passes.
5. Refactor the code as needed.
6. Repeat steps *2* through *5* as needed.

We can use React Testing Library to drive the development of React components using the TDD approach. First, we will use TDD to build the Vote component we introduced in a previous section in this chapter. Then, we will use TDD to create a Registration component.

Building the Vote component using TDD

In the *Testing components that call event handlers in isolation* section, we built a `Vote Button` component by first building the component and then writing tests. In this section, we will use TDD to build the component. First, we plan out how the component should look when rendered into the DOM and the actions a user should take. We decide the component will be an image button. The parent component should pass the image source and image alt text into the component as `props`.

The component will also accept a Boolean value passed for the `hasVoted` prop to set the button's state to `enabled` or `disabled`. If `hasVoted` is set to `true`, a user can click the button to invoke a method that will handle updating the vote count. Next, we write tests based on our design. The first test will verify the component renders to the screen with the `props` passed in:

```
test('given image and vote status, renders button to
  screen', () => {
  const stubHandleVote = jest.fn()
  const stubAltText = 'vote like'

  render(
    <VoteBtn
      handleVote={stubHandleVote}
      hasVoted={false}
      imgSrc={stubThumbsUp}
      altText={stubAltText}
    />
  )
  const image = screen.getByRole('img', { name:
    stubAltText })
  const button = screen.getByRole('button', { name:
    stubAltText })
```

In the preceding code, first, we create `jest` functions and assign them to the `stubHandleVote` and `stubAltText` variables. We prepend the variable names with *stub* because we are only using them as dependency placeholders in the test. The variable names also provide more context for their purpose in the test.

Next, we render the component with `props` values passed in. Then, we grab the `image` and `button` elements and assign them to associated variables. Next, we will make assertions:

```
    expect(image).toBeInTheDocument()
    expect(button).toBeInTheDocument()
    expect(button).toBeEnabled()
})
```

In the preceding code, we assert that the `image` and `button` elements are on the DOM. We also assert that the button state is `enabled`, meaning a user can click it. We create a file for the `Vote Button` component like so:

```
const VoteBtn = props => {
    return null
}
export default VoteBtn
```

We create a `VoteBtn` component that doesn't currently return any code to render in the DOM in the preceding code. We also export the component to be used in other files. When we run the test, we get the following output from the test results:

Figure 3.17 – TDD Vote Button test step 1

In the preceding screenshot, the **given image and vote status, renders button to screen** test failed. The failure output provides context for the failure that occurred when the test did not find an `image` element with the name `vote like` in the DOM. Since we know the image should be a child of a `button` element, next we will resolve the error by creating the `button` element with a child `image` element and pass in the required properties in the `VoteBtn` component file:

```
const VoteBtn = props => {
    return (
        <button disabled={props.hasVoted}>
            <img src={props.imgSrc} alt={props.altText} />
        </button>
    )
```

```
}
export default VoteBtn
```

In the previous code, we create a `button` element with the child `image` element and required `props` for the image source, alt text, and disabled attributes. Now when we run our test, we receive the following output:

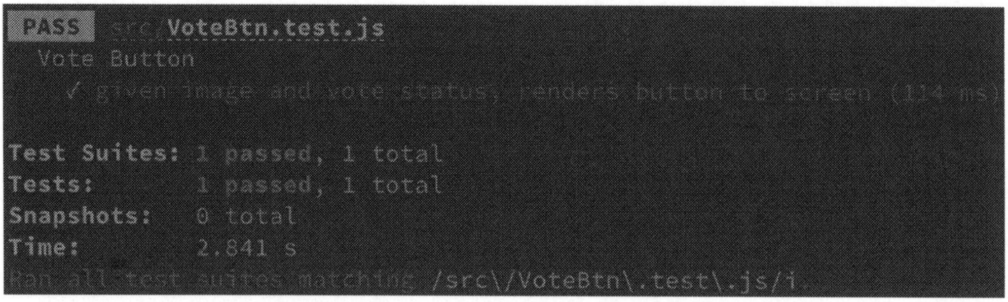

```
PASS  src/VoteBtn.test.js
  Vote Button
    ✓ given image and vote status, renders button to screen (114 ms)


Test Suites: 1 passed, 1 total
Tests:       1 passed, 1 total
Snapshots:   0 total
Time:        2.841 s
Ran all test suites matching /src\/VoteBtn\.test\.js/i.
```

Figure 3.18 – TDD Vote Button test step 2

In the preceding screenshot, the **given image and vote status, renders button to screen** test now passes. For the next piece of `Vote Button`, we will write the code allowing a user to click the button to invoke a method that will handle updating the vote count when `hasVoted` is set to `true`. First, we will create another test to target the functionality:

```
test('given clicked button, invokes handleVote', () => {
  const mockHandleVote = jest.fn()
  render(
    <VoteBtn
      handleVote={mockHandleVote}
      hasVoted={false}
      imgSrc={stubThumbsUp}
      altText="vote like"
    />
  )
```

In the preceding code, first, we create a `jest` function and assign it to the variable named `mockHandleVote`. We prepend the variable name with *mock* because we will assert against the variable later in the test. Next, we render the `VoteBtn` component into the DOM and pass in the required properties. Notice that we pass in `mockHandleVote` for the `handleVote` property. Next, we will click the button and make assertions:

```
user.click(screen.getByRole('button', { name: /vote
    like/i }))


  expect(mockHandleVote).toHaveBeenCalled()
  expect(mockHandleVote).toHaveBeenCalledTimes(1)
})
```

In the preceding code, first, we click the button inside the component. Then, we assert that `mockHandleVote` was called and called precisely one time. Verifying if and how `mockHandleVote` was called is essential. If `mockHandleVote` is not called or is called more than once per click, we know the component will not correctly communicate when integrated with the parent component. We receive the following output when we run the test:

```
FAIL  src/VoteBtn.test.js
Vote Button
  × given clicked button, invokes handleVote (128 ms)


  ● Vote Button › given clicked button, invokes handleVote

    expect(jest.fn()).toHaveBeenCalled()

    Expected number of calls: >= 1
    Received number of calls:    0

        user.click(screen.getByRole('button', { name: /vote like/i }))
```

Figure 3.19 – TDD Vote Button test step 3

In the preceding code, the **given clicked button, invokes handleVote** test fails. The test expected the `jest` function passed in the component to be called at least once, but it was never called. Next, we will resolve the error by adding the implementation to the component:

```
<button onClick={props.handleVote} disabled={props.
    hasVoted}>
```

In the preceding code, we added an `onClick` event handler that will invoke the `handleVote` method passed into the component as a property when the button is clicked. Now when we run the test, we get the following output:

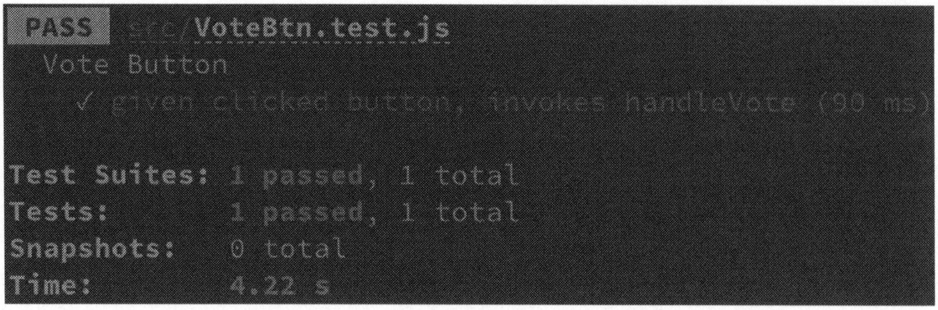

Figure 3.20 – TDD Vote Button test step 4

In the preceding screenshot, the **given clicked button, invokes handleVote** test passes. Now that all our design plans for `Vote Button` have been implemented and tested, we have finished building the feature using the TDD approach.

In the next section, we will use TDD to create a registration component.

Building a registration form using TDD

In the previous section, we used TDD to build a `Vote` component. In this section, we will use TDD to build a component used to create user accounts for a website. Then, once we build the minimal functionality to make the test pass, we will also refactor the component's implementation and verify the test continues to pass. The component will have a **Register here** heading element, `email` and `password` fields, and a **Submit** button. When the form is submitted, a `handleSubmit` method should be invoked. The final version of the component should look like the following:

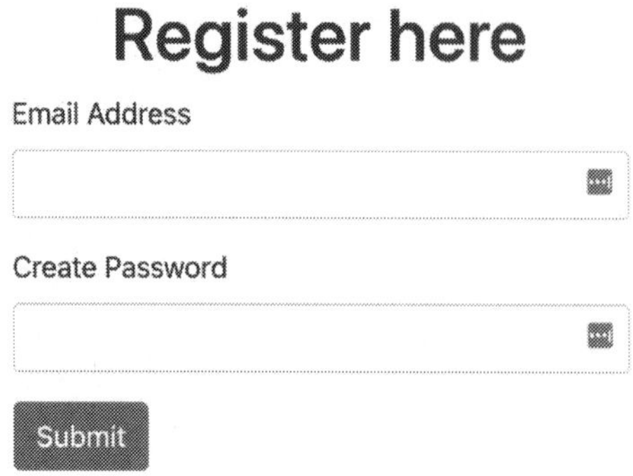

Figure 3.21 – Registration form

In the preceding screenshot, we have a form allowing users to submit an email and password to register an account for a website. Now that we understand how the final version should look on the screen, we will write a test based on our design. For purposes of this section, we will verify that a `handleRegister` method is called when the form is submitted:

```
test('given submitted form, invokes handleRegister', ()
 => {
  const mockHandleRegister = jest.fn()
  const mockValues = {
    email: 'john@mail.com',
    password: '123'
  }

  render(<Register handleRegister={mockHandleRegister} />)
```

In the preceding code, we create `mockHandleRegister` and `mockValues` variables. The variables will be asserted against later in the test. Then, we render the component under test into the DOM and pass in `mockHandleRegister`. Now, `mockHandleRegister` will allow us to test the `Register` component in isolation from the `handleRegister` dependency. Next, we will enter values in the form fields:

```
user.type(screen.getByLabelText('Email Address'),
  mockValues.email)
user.type(screen.getByLabelText('Create Password'),
  mockValues.password)
user.click(screen.getByRole('button', { name: /submit/i }))
```

In the preceding code, we enter values from the `mockValues` object into the `email` and `password` fields. Notice the use of string values passed into the `getByLabelText` queries. String values are another option for queries when you do not want to use a regular expression. Next, we will make assertions:

```
  expect(mockHandleRegister).toHaveBeenCalledTimes(1)
  expect(mockHandleRegister).toHaveBeenCalledWith({
    email: mockValues.email,
    password: mockValues.password
  })
})
```

In the preceding code, we expect `mockHandleRegister` to be called once. Finally, we expect values from the `mockValues` object to have been included as arguments when `mockHandleRegister` was called. Verifying the arguments passed to `mockHandleRegister` is important because it helps reduce the risk that form values will not be passed to `handleRegister`.

Next, we will create a file for the `Register` component like so:

```
export default class Register extends React.Component {
  render() {
    return null
  }
}
```

We create and export a `Register` component that doesn't currently return any code to render in the DOM in the preceding code. When we run the test, we get the following output from the test results:

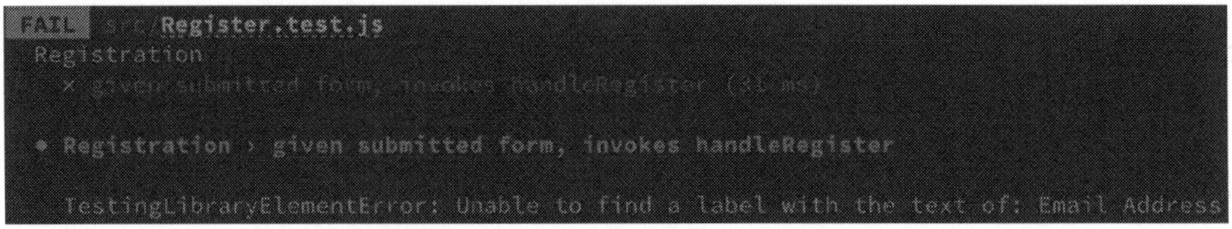

Figure 3.22 – TDD registration test step 1

In the preceding screenshot, the **given submitted form, invokes handleRegister** test failed. The failure output provides context for the failure that occurred when the test did not find an `email` field element in the DOM. Next, we will resolve the error by creating the `email` field. We will also create the `password` field and the **Submit** button:

```
  state = {
    email: '',
    password: ''
  }

  handleChange = event => {
    const { id, value } = event.target
    this.setState(prevState => {
      return {
        ...prevState,
```

```
            [id]: value
        }
    })
  }
```

In the preceding code, first, we create a `state` object to store values entered for the `email` and `password` fields. Next, we create a `handleChange` method that will be called anytime a user enters a value into a form field. The `handleChange` method will update `state` values based on the `form` field that is changed. Next, we create the `heading` element and an `email` field:

```
<main>
  <h1>Register here</h1>
  <form>
    <div>
      <label htmlFor='email'>Email Address</label>
      <input
        value={this.state.email}
        onChange={this.handleChange}
        type='email'
        id='email'
      />
    </div>
```

In the preceding code, first, we create a `main` element to wrap the `heading` and `form` elements. Inside `main`, we create the **Register here** heading. Then, we create a `form` element and add a field for users to enter an email address. When a user enters a value into the field, an `onChange` event handler is invoked to call `handleChange` to update the state object's associated value. The field's `value` attribute always displays the current value stored in the state object's associated key. Next, we will create a field for users to enter a password and a `button` element to submit the form:

```
    <div>
      <label htmlFor='password'>Create Password
      </label>
      <input
        value={this.state.password}
        onChange={this.handleChange}
        type='password'
```

```
            id='password'
        />
    </div>
    <button type='submit'>Submit</button>
</form>
</main>
```

In the preceding code, first, we create a `password` field. The field has the same event handler methods as the `email` field. Finally, we make a **Submit** button to allow a user to submit values entered in the form. Now when we run the test, we get the following output:

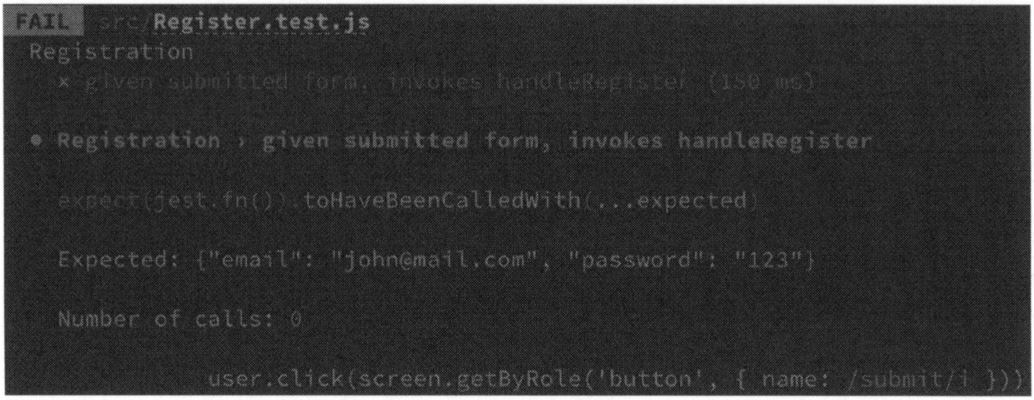

Figure 3.23 – TDD registration test step 2

In the preceding code, our test is still failing, but for a different reason. Now the test can enter values and submit the form, but `mockHandleRegister` was not called with the submitted values. The failure happened because we have not yet implemented an `onSubmit` event handler to call our `mockHandleRegister` method and any other desired behavior when the form is submitted.

Next, we will resolve the error by adding an `onSubmit` handler to the form and have it call a `handleSubmit` method that we will create:

```
handleSubmit = event => {
    event.preventDefault()
    this.props.handleRegister(this.state)
}
```

In the preceding code, we create the `handleSubmit` method. When `handleSubmit` is invoked, the browser `event` that triggered the method is passed into it. Next, we prevent the browser's normal behavior of refreshing the page after submitting a form using the `preventDefault` method. Finally, we call `handleRegister`, provided to the component as `props`, and pass in the form values stored in the `state` object. Next, we will attach `handleSubmit` to the form:

```
<form onSubmit={this.handleSubmit}>
```

In the preceding code, we add an `onSubmit` event handler and pass in `handleSubmit`. When the form is submitted, `handleSubmit` will be called, resulting in `handleRegister` being called, with the form values as arguments. Now when we run the test, we get the following output:

```
PASS  src/Register.test.js
  Registration
    ✓ given submitted form, invokes handleRegister (158 ms)

Test Suites: 1 passed, 1 total
Tests:       1 passed, 1 total
Snapshots:   0 total
Time:        2.015 s
```

Figure 3.24 – TDD registration test step 3

The preceding screenshot shows that our test is finally passing. Technically, we could stop here since our code makes our test pass. However, we can make our component code cleaner by converting it from a class component into a function component. As long as the behavior remains the same, our test should continue to pass. We can refactor the component like so:

```
const Register = props => {
  const [values, setValues] = React.useState({
    email: '',
    password: ''
  })
```

In the preceding code, first, we convert the class into a function. Then, we use the `useState` hook to manage the form value state. Next, we will refactor our `handleChange` and `handleSubmit` methods:

```
const handleChange = event => {
  const { id, value } = event.target
  setValues({ ...values, [id]: value })
}
const handleSubmit = event => {
  event.preventDefault()
  props.handleRegister(values)
}
```

In the previous code, the `handleChange` class and `handleSubmit` methods are converted to function expressions. The `handleChange` method calls `setValues` to update the state for each entered form value. The implementation of `handleSubmit` is virtually the same as the class version. Next, we will refactor the returned code that renders as HTML in the browser:

```
<main className="m-3 d-flex flex-column">
    <h1>Register here</h1>
    <form onSubmit={handleSubmit}>
      <div>
        <label htmlFor="email">Email Address</label>
        <input
          value={values.email}
          onChange={handleChange}
// the rest of the component code ...
```

In the preceding code, first, we remove the `render` method required in `class` components. The remainder of the code is very similar to the class version. However, the `value` attribute uses the `values` object, and the `handleChange` method passed in to the `onChange` event handler does not need to include the `this` keyword. When we rerun our test, we get the following result:

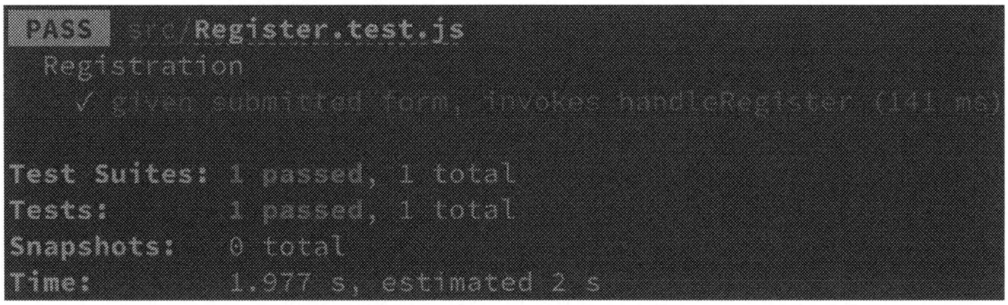

Figure 3.25 – TDD registration test step 4

In the preceding screenshot, our test still passes after the refactor. The `refactor` component made our code a lot cleaner. Now you understand how to build a component using TDD with React Testing Library. In this section, we used TDD to drive the creation of vote and registration features. The test result feedback that React Testing Library provides makes for a pleasant experience to guide development.

Summary

In this chapter, you learned how to install and use a module to simulate user actions on the resulting DOM output for components. You can now install and test features that interact with APIs with a user-friendly tool. You understand how to test components in isolation from event handler dependencies with mock functions. Finally, you learned how to implement the TDD approach to building features combined with React Testing Library.

In the next chapter, we will dive deeper by learning the benefits of integration testing. We will also learn how to test React components that utilize popular third-party libraries.

Questions

1. Why should you favor `user-event` over `fireEvent` to simulate user actions in your tests?

2. Explain how MSW allows you to test components that make requests to APIs.

3. What is a mock function?

4. Explain the application risk associated with testing components in isolation with mock functions.

5. In your own words, describe the TDD workflow.

6. Explain when to use a `getBy*`, `findBy*`, or `queryBy*` query to select an element.

4

Integration Testing and Third-Party Libraries in Your Application

In previous chapters, we learned how to test components in isolation separate from dependencies. We also learned how to test components that manage state. In many applications, teams can increase velocity by incorporating third-party tools to manage state and build components. By the end of this chapter, you will have learned about the benefits of using the integration approach to testing. You will understand how to configure tests to make assertions against components using advanced state management tools. You will learn how to test for errors rendered in applications. You will test components that interact with API servers that structure data differently from traditional **Representational State Transfer (REST)** APIs by allowing you to describe and receive only the specific data needed by your frontend application. Finally, you will learn how to test components that use a popular React component library.

In this chapter, we're going to cover the following main topics:

- Gaining value with integration testing
- Testing components that use the Context API

- Testing components that use Redux
- Testing components that use GraphQL
- Testing components built with Material-UI

The skills gained in this chapter will deepen our understanding of testing React components in various scenarios.

Technical requirements

For the examples in this chapter, you will need to have Node.js installed on your machine. We will be using the `create-react-app` CLI tool for all code examples. Please familiarize yourself with the tool before starting the chapter if needed. Also, you will need to have a basic understanding of Redux and the React Context API. Code snippets will be provided throughout the chapter to help you understand the code under test, but the objective is understanding how to test the code. You can find code examples for this chapter here: `https://github.com/PacktPublishing/Simplify-Testing-with-React-Testing-Library/tree/master/Chapter04`.

Testing integrated components

In the previous chapter, we learned how to test components in isolation from dependencies, including other components. Isolated testing has its advantages but also has drawbacks because real dependencies are replaced with test doubles. In this section, we will learn how to test components that integrate with other components. In many scenarios, integration testing can add more value than isolated testing because we can test the code in ways that are closer to its production use. We can also add test coverage faster for components because one test can cover multiple components at once. We will use integration testing in a few examples in this section.

Using integration testing with the Vote component

In the previous chapter, we tested the `Vote` component, which allowed users to click a button to increase or decrease the total likes. In this section, we will break up the implementation into separate components and write integration tests. The component included two `button` elements:

```
<button
    onClick={handleLikeVote}
    disabled={hasVoted}
    style={clickedLike ? { background: 'green' } : null}
```

```
    >
        <img src={thumbsUp} alt="thumbs up" />
    </button>
    <div>{totalLikes}</div>
    <button
        onClick={handleDislikeVote}
        disabled={hasVoted}
        style={clickedDislike ? { background: 'red' } : null}
    >
        <img src={thumbsDown} alt="thumbs down" />
    </button>
```

In the previous code, the properties for the two button elements are very similar and could be extracted into their own component files to be reusable in other parts of the application:

```
const VoteBtn = props => {
    return (
        <button onClick={props.handleVote} disabled={props.
            hasVoted}>
            <img src={props.imgSrc} alt={props.altText} />
        </button>
    )
}
```

In the previous code, we have a VoteBtn component created in its own file that can be reused anywhere throughout the application. VoteBtn can be used inside the Vote component to replace the hardcoded button element:

```
return (
    <div className="h1">
        <h5>Note: You are not allowed to change your vote once
            selected!</h5>
        <VoteBtn
            handleVote={handleVoteLike}
            hasVoted={hasVoted}
            imgSrc={thumbsUp}
            altText="thumbs up"
        />
```

```
    <div>{totalLikes}</div>
    <VoteBtn
      handleVote={handleVoteDislike}
      hasVoted={hasVoted}
      imgSrc={thumbsDown}
      altText="thumbs down"
    />
  </div>
)
```

In the previous code, two instances of `VoteBtn` are integrated into the `Vote` component. We could test `VoteBtn` in isolation from the `Vote` component, but we can gain more value by testing the integration of the two together. For the first test, we can verify that an `"up"` vote increases the sum of total likes by one:

```
test('given "up" vote, total likes increases by one', () => {
  render(<Vote totalGlobalLikes={10} />)

  user.click(screen.getByRole('button', { name: /thumbs up/i
}))

  expect(screen.getByText(/11/i)).toBeInTheDocument()
})
```

In the previous code, first, we rendered the `Vote` component into the DOM with a value of `10` passed into the `totalGlobalLikes` property. Next, we click the **thumbs up** button. Finally, we assert that the number `11` in is the DOM. For the next test, we will verify that a `"down"` vote decreases the sum of total likes by one:

```
test('given "down" vote, total likes decreases by one', () =>
{
  render(<Vote totalGlobalLikes={10} />)

  user.click(screen.getByRole('button', { name: /thumbs
    down/i }))

  expect(screen.getByText(/9/i)).toBeInTheDocument()
})
```

In the previous example, the code is similar to that in the first example. The only difference is instead of clicking the **thumbs up** button, we click the **thumbs down** button. Then, after performing the button click, we assert that the number 9 is in the DOM. The last test we will write will verify that a user can only vote once:

```
test('given vote, returns disabled vote buttons', () => {
    render(<Vote totalGlobalLikes={10} />)
    const thumbsUpBtn = screen.getByRole('button', { name: /
        thumbs up/i })
    const thumbsDownBtn = screen.getByRole('button', { name: /
        thumbs down/i })

    user.click(thumbsUpBtn)
    user.click(thumbsUpBtn)
    user.click(thumbsDownBtn)
    user.click(thumbsDownBtn)

    expect(screen.getByText(/11/i)).toBeInTheDocument()
})
```

In the previous code, first, we rendered the Vote component into the DOM with a value of 10 passed into the totalGlobalLikes property. Next, we grab the **thumbs up** and **thumbs down** buttons and place them in variables. The buttons are placed in variables to make the test code cleaner since they will be used multiple times in the test. Then, we click both buttons numerous times. Finally, we assert that the number 11 is in the DOM. The number 11 is expected because the **thumbs up** button was clicked first, which disables the buttons. By using the integration testing approach, we were able to verify the outcome of the total likes displayed on the screen and the state of buttons after simulating click events all in the same test.

When we run all the `Vote` component tests, we get the following output:

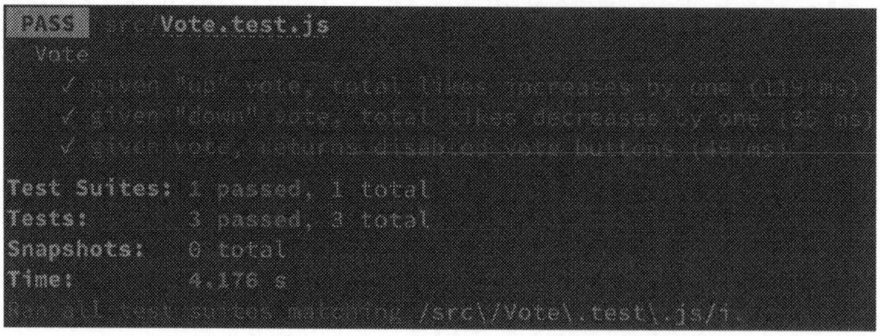

Figure 4.1 – Vote component test results

The preceding screenshot shows that tests **given "up" vote, total likes increases by one**, **given "down" vote, total likes decreases by one**, and **given vote, returns disabled vote buttons** all passed in the `Vote.test.js` file.

Now you understand the advantages of testing components integrated with dependencies. However, there are scenarios where using the integrated approach may not be the best strategy. In the next section, we will look at a scenario where testing a component in isolation would provide more value than integration testing.

Planning test scenarios better suited for isolated testing

In the previous section, we learned the advantages of testing components integrated with dependencies. However, there are some scenarios where using the isolated testing approach is a better fit. In the *Implementing test-driven development* section of *Chapter 3, Testing Complex Components with React Testing Library*, we built a registration form. As a reference, the output of the component was as follows:

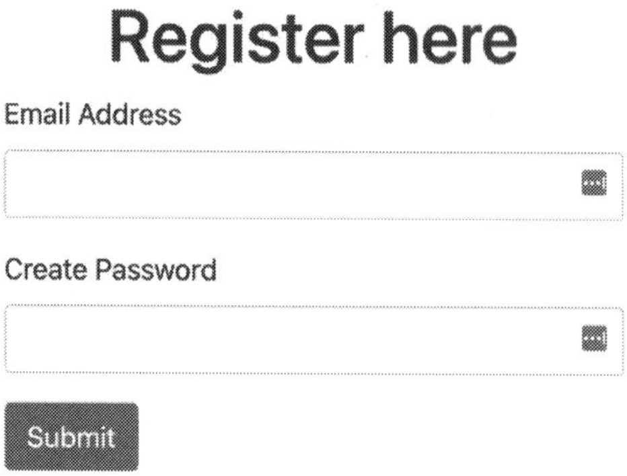

Figure 4.2 – Registration form

In the preceding screenshot, we see the registration component that allows a user to submit an email address and password. The test used the isolated approach and verified the happy path of invoking a `handleRegister` method when the form is submitted. Let's say a new feature is added where a success message is sent to the frontend from the server and replaces the form on the screen when registration is successful:

Register here

Registration Successful!

Figure 4.3 – Registration success

In the preceding screenshot, the message **Registration Successful!** is displayed after successful form submission. Verifying the message is on the screen after submitting the form could be tested using the integration approach but might be a slow-running test. We could create a faster running isolated test by creating a mock server response. What about scenarios where form validation errors are displayed and prevent users from submitting the form? For example, form validation errors could be displayed when a user enters an invalid email or attempts to submit the form with blank fields. The password field could also present several test scenarios, such as displaying errors when the minimal password length is not met, or special characters are not included in the password.

The previous scenarios are all good use cases for the isolated test approach. The errors displayed on the screen do not depend on any code outside the component. We can test various combinations in the form and edge cases that will run extremely fast and quickly add a lot of value. In general, consider creating an isolated test for scenarios where a test setup using the integrated approach would prove cumbersome or when the integration approach yields slow-running tests. Also, keep in mind how many dependencies have to be mocked when creating an isolated test. Mocking multiple dependencies provides less value than testing with dependencies included.

Now you know how to test components integrated with dependencies. You understand the benefits of integration testing compared to testing in isolation. You also know that in some scenarios, testing a component using the isolated approach can yield better outcomes for your testing plan than solely using the integrated approach. The decision to test a component in isolation or integrated with dependencies will depend on your test plans. In the next section, we will visit more examples using the isolated and integrated testing approach and learn how to test components that use the Context API for state management.

Testing components that use the Context API

In this section, we will learn how to test components that use the React library's **Context API** to manage state. The Context API helps solve issues related to passing props and methods multiple levels down the component tree, similar to Redux. The Context API allows you to directly send data to consumers without traveling through numerous parent-level components to get to the target consumer. An example application where the state could be more easily managed with the Context API is a website that allows users to change the theme from light to dark because multiple components would need to be aware when the theme changes. Another example would be a complex social networking site such as Twitter. Components that use Context must be used within the `Context Provider` component:

```
import { LikesProvider } from './LikesContext'
import Vote from './Vote'

const App = () => (
    <LikesProvider initialLikes={10}>
        <Vote />
    </LikesProvider>
)
```

In the preceding code, the `LikesProvider` component, responsible for providing the Context state to Context consumers, is rendered with `Vote` as a child component. `LikesProvider` provides all the consuming components with an `initialLikes` count of `10`. Since `Vote` is rendered within `LikesProvider`, it can view and update state provided by `LikesProvider`. To test the `Context Provider` component's consumers, we need a way to access `Context Provider` within our tests. We will use a retail application to demonstrate how to implement the requirements.

Testing a context consuming Retail component

In this section, we will test a `Retail` component that consumes state provided by a `RetailContext` component. The UI of the `Retail` component looks as follows:

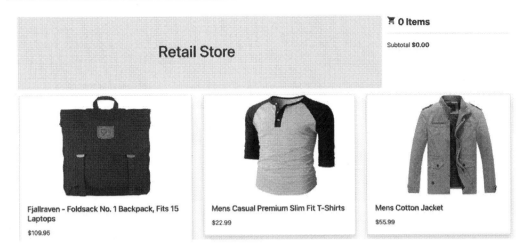

Figure 4.4 – Retail component UI

The preceding screenshot shows the initial screen output of the `Retail` component. A list of clothing products and a shopping cart is shown. There is also a section with the text **Retail Store** that will display product details once clicked:

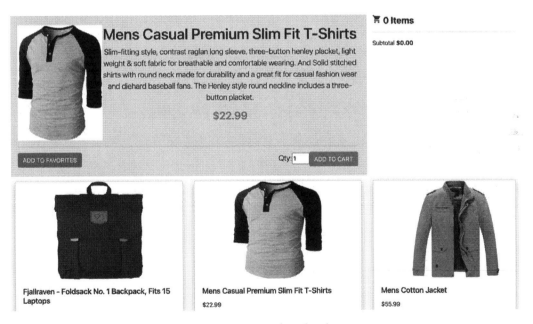

Figure 4.5 – Product details

The preceding screenshot shows details for **Mens Casual Premium Slim Fit T-Shirts** after being clicked by the user. A user can click the **ADD TO FAVORITES** button to *favorite* the item:

Figure 4.6 –Favorited product details

The preceding screenshot shows that the text **ADD TO FAVORITES** changes to **ADDED TO FAVORITES** once the button is clicked. Finally, a user can add a quantity and click the **ADD TO CART** button to add the product to their cart:

Figure 4.7 – Product added to cart

The preceding screenshot shows a quantity of **3** of the item **Mens Casual Premium Slim Fit T-Shirts** added to the cart. The cart displays **1 Items**, representing the total items in the cart. The cart also shows the **Subtotal** for all items added to the cart.

In the code implementation, the `Retail` component is rendered as a child component of `RetailProvider` inside `App`:

```
import retailProducts from './api/retailProducts'
import Retail from './Retail'
import { RetailProvider } from './RetailContext'

const App = () => (
  <RetailProvider products={retailProducts}>
    <Retail />
  </RetailProvider>
)
```

In the preceding code, `RetailProvider` receives an array of products via `retailProducts`. The `retailProducts` data is a local subset of data from the Fake Store API (`https://fakestoreapi.com`) API, a free open source REST API that provides sample products. The `Retail` component includes three separate child components – `ProductList`, `ProductDetail`, and `Cart` – that integrate together to consume and manage `RetailContext` state:

```
const Retail = () => {
  return (
    <div className="container-fluid">
      <div className="row mt-3">
        <ProductDetail />
        <Cart />
      </div>

      <ProductList />
    </div>
  )
}
```

The `Retail` component renders the `ProductList`, `ProductDetail`, and `Cart` components as child components inside `div` elements in the preceding code.

We will use a combination of isolated unit tests and integration tests to verify that the `Retail` code works as expected.

Testing the Cart component in isolation

In this section, we will verify the initial state of the `Cart` component. We will use a unit test approach because the initial state depends on `RetailContext` and not other `Retail` components:

```
test('Cart, given initial render, returns empty cart', () => {
  render(
    <RetailProvider products={testProducts}>
      <Cart />
    </RetailProvider>
  )

  expect(screen.getByText(/0 items/i)).toBeInTheDocument()
  expect(screen.getByText(/\$0\.00/i)).toBeInTheDocument()
})
```

In the previous code, we first render the `Cart` component as a child of `RetailProvider`. Next, we make two assertions. First, we assert the text `0 items` is in the DOM. Then, we assert the text `$0.00` is in the DOM. When we run the test for the `Cart` component, we get the following output:

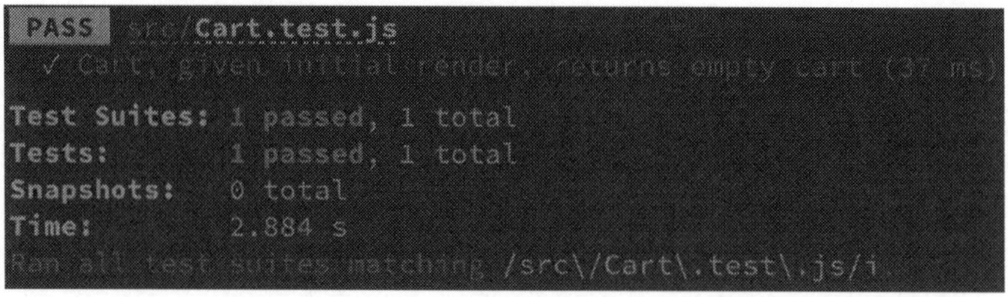

Figure 4.8 – Cart component test result

The preceding screenshot shows the test **Cart, given initial render, returns empty cart** passes. Now we have a test verifying the initial state of the `Cart` component.

In the next section, we will test the `Product` component.

Testing the Product component in isolation

In this section, we will verify the `Product` component can display passed-in product data to the DOM. We will use `faker`, a popular library, to generate test data. We can write the following test:

```
test('Product, given product properties, renders to screen', ()
=> {
  const product = {
    title: faker.commerce.productName(),
    price: faker.commerce.price(),
    image: faker.image.fashion()
  }
```

In the previous code snippet, we use `faker` to generate random `productName`, `price`, and `fashion image` data for our test. Using `faker` to generate our test data automatically, we can eliminate any confusion for new team members looking at our code to learn about the component under test. A new team member may see hardcoded data and think the component must have that specific data to work properly. Random data created by `faker` can make it clearer that the component does not need to be specifically hardcoded to function as expected. Next, we write the remaining code for the test:

```
  render(
    <RetailProvider products={testProducts}>
      <Product
        title={product.title}
        price={product.price}
        image={product.image}
      />
    </RetailProvider>
  )

  expect(screen.getByText(product.title)).toBeInTheDocument()
  expect(screen.getByText(`$${product.price}`)).
    toBeInTheDocument()
})
```

In the previous code snippet, we wrap the `Product` component inside `RetailProvider`, pass in test data as props, and render the DOM component. Finally, assert that the product `title` and `price` is in the DOM. Now we have verified that the `Product` component accepts and renders prop data into the DOM as expected. When we run the test for the `Product` component, we get the following output:

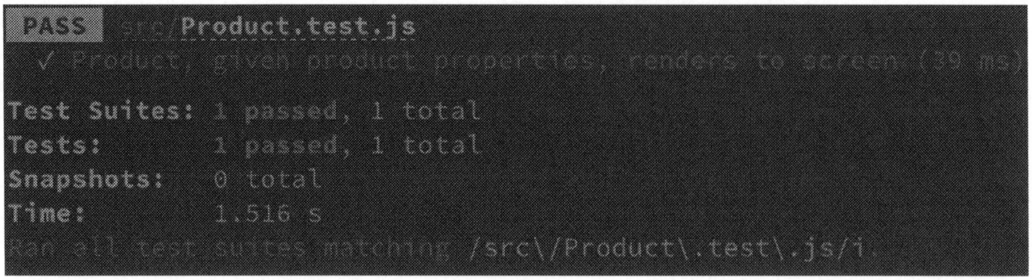

Figure 4.9 – Product component test result

The preceding screenshot shows the test **Product, given product properties, renders to screen** passes. Now we have verified the `Product` component correctly displays passed in data to the screen.

Next, we will test the `ProductDetail` component.

Testing the ProductDetail component in isolation

This section will verify that `ProductDetail` initially renders the text **Retail Store** into the DOM. The **Retail Store** text serves as a placeholder until a user clicks one of the products. We can test the component as follows:

```
test('ProductDetail, given initial render, displays Placeholder
  component', () => {
  render(
    <RetailProvider products={testProducts}>
      <ProductDetail />
    </RetailProvider>
  )

  expect(
    screen.getByRole('heading', { name: /retail store/i })
  ).toBeInTheDocument()
})
```

In the preceding code, we wrap `ProductDetail` inside `RetailProvider`. Then, we assert that the text **Retail Store** is in the DOM. Running the test results in the following output:

```
PASS    src   ProductDetail.test.js
  ✓ ProductDetail, given initial render, displays Placeholder component (12 ms)

Test Suites: 1 passed, 1 total
Tests:       1 passed, 1 total
Snapshots:   0 total
Time:        1.71 s
Ran all test suites matching /src\/ProductDetail\.test\.js/i
```

Figure 4.10 – ProductDetail component test result

The preceding screenshot shows the test **ProductDetail, given initial render, displays Placeholder component** passes as expected. Now we know that `ProductDetail` renders the correct text on the initial render.

Next, we will verify the error displayed when a consumer is used outside of `Context Provider`.

Testing context errors using error boundaries

In this section, we will verify that the `Retail` component must be wrapped in `RetailProvider` before using it in the first test. This test is important because the `Retail` component cannot work as expected without the stateful data provided by `RetailContext`. Inside the `RetailContext` code, we have a check to make sure the methods used to access `RetailContext` are used within `Provider`:

```
function useRetail() {
    const context = React.useContext(RetailContext)

    if (!context) {
        throw new Error('useRetail must be used within the
            RetailProvider')
    }
}
```

In the previous code snippet, if a user attempts to use the `useRetail` method to access `RetailContent`'s stateful data outside of `RetailProvider`, a *throw error* will occur and stop the application from running. We can write the test as follows:

```
test('Retail must be rendered within Context Provider', () => {
    jest.spyOn(console, 'error').mockImplementation(() => {})
```

```
const ErrorFallback = ({ error }) => error.message

render(
  <ErrorBoundary FallbackComponent={ErrorFallback}>
    <Retail />
  </ErrorBoundary>
)
```

In the preceding code, we use the jest.spyOn method to keep an eye on the console.log method throughout the test. We also attach an empty callback method as mockImplementation. We use mockImplementation to control what happens when console.error is called. We don't want anything specific logged to the console in our test results related to the console for this test.error execution, so we pass in the empty callback function.

Next, we create ErrorFallback, a component we will use to receive the message included in the error thrown by RetailContext. Next, we wrap Retail in ErrorBoundary, which gives us control over errors thrown by components. We can manually create an error boundary component but react-error-boundary (https://github.com/bvaughn/react-error-boundary) provides an easy-to-use error boundary component. We provide ErrorFallback as the value for FallbackComponent. When Retail is rendered, and the error is thrown, the ErrorBoundary component will pass the error on to ErrorFallback.

Next, we perform assertions:

```
const errorMessage = screen.getByText(/must be used within the
  RetailProvider/i)
  expect(errorMessage).toBeInTheDocument()


  expect(console.error).toHaveBeenCalled()
  console.error.mockRestore()
})
```

In the preceding code, first, we query the DOM for the error message must be used within the RetailProvider. Next, we expect console.error to have been called. Finally, as a test clean-up step, we restore console.error back to its original state, allowing it to be called wherever necessary for successive tests. Now you know how to verify that a context-consuming component cannot be rendered outside of Context Provider.

Using integration testing to test view product details

For our next test, we will verify that a user can click a product and see product details. The steps involved in viewing a product's details is a user workflow that would be good to test using the integration approach. We can write the test as follows:

```
test('A user can view product details', () => {
  render(
    <RetailProvider products={testProducts}>
      <Retail />
    </RetailProvider>
  )
  const firstProduct = testProducts[0]

  user.click(
    screen.getByRole('heading', {
      name: firstProduct.title
    })
  )
```

In the preceding code, we wrap the `Retail` component in `RetailProvider` and render it in the DOM. Next, we grab the first item in the `testProducts` array and assign it to the variable `firstProduct`. Then, we click the `title` of the first product on the screen. Finally, we assert the output:

```
  expect(
    screen.getAllByRole('heading', { name: firstProduct.title
      }).length
  ).toEqual(2)
  expect(screen.getByText(firstProduct.description)).
    toBeInTheDocument()
  expect(
    screen.getByRole('heading', { name: `$${firstProduct.
      price}` })
  ).toBeInTheDocument()
})
```

In the preceding code, we assert the first product's title is displayed twice on the screen. Finally, we assert the product's `description` and `price` data is displayed on the screen.

For our next test, we will verify that a user can add a product to the cart. We can write the following test code:

```
function addFirstItemToCart() {
  const firstProduct = testProducts[1]
  const firstProductTitle = screen.getByRole('heading', {
    name: firstProduct.title
  })

  user.click(firstProductTitle)
  user.click(screen.getByRole('button', { name: /add to
    cart/i }))
}
```

In the previous code snippet, we create an `addFirstItemToCart` function to execute the same test steps in successive tests and avoid code duplication. Next, we write the main test code:

```
test('A user can add a product to the cart', () => {
  render(
    <RetailProvider products={testProducts}>
      <Retail />
    </RetailProvider>
  )
  addFirstItemToCart()

  expect(screen.getByText(/1 items/i)).toBeInTheDocument()
})
```

In the previous code, we render the `Retail` component inside `RetailProvider`. Next, we execute the `addFirstItemToCart` method. Finally, we assert that the text `1 items` is in the DOM. Now we are confident a user can add an item to the cart using `Retail` integrated with the `Product`, `ProductDetail`, and `Cart` components.

As a challenge, try to write the code for the following test scenarios: **A user can update the quantity for cart items, A user cannot submit a quantity greater than 10, A user cannot submit a quantity less than 1**, and **A user can add an item to favorites**. The solutions for these test scenarios can be found in the *Chapter 4 code samples* (`https://github.com/PacktPublishing/Simplify-Testing-with-React-Testing-Library/tree/master/Chapter04/ch_04_context`). Now you know how to write integration tests for components that use the Context API. You have a better understanding of unit testing components in isolation through multiple examples. You also know how to test for errors thrown using error boundaries.

This section's learnings will be beneficial in the next section when we learn how to test components that manage state using Redux. There will be a few differences, but similar strategies from this section will be used in general.

Testing components that use Redux

This section will teach you how to test components that use the popular **Redux** library to manage the application state. The strategies used in this section will be very similar to those used in the previous section, with a few differences. While testing components using the Context API in the last section, we learned that those components must be used within `Context Provider`.

To test components using Redux, components must be used within the Redux state providing context:

```
ReactDOM.render(
  <Provider store={store}>
    <App />
  </Provider>,
  document.getElementById('root')
)
```

In the preceding code, we have a top-level App passed in as a child component of the Redux `Provider` component. Wrapping the top-level App component is a common pattern in Redux that allows any child component in the application to access the stateful data provided by Redux. Stateful data and methods to modify state are passed to the Provider's `store` property. Typically, you will create this code in separate files, wire everything together using Redux's API methods, and pass the combined result to the `store` property.

When designing Redux-consuming component tests, we need to pass in test data that we can use as the Redux state. Simply passing in test data to the `store` property of the Redux Provider will not work because we also need to include the Redux methods used to consume and update the stateful data:

```
test('Cart, given initial render, displays empty cart', () => {
  render(
    <Provider store={'some test data'}>
      <Cart />
    </Provider>
  )
```

In the previous code snippet, we have a `Cart` component test that passes in the string **some test data** as test data to the Redux store. When we run the test, we receive the following output:

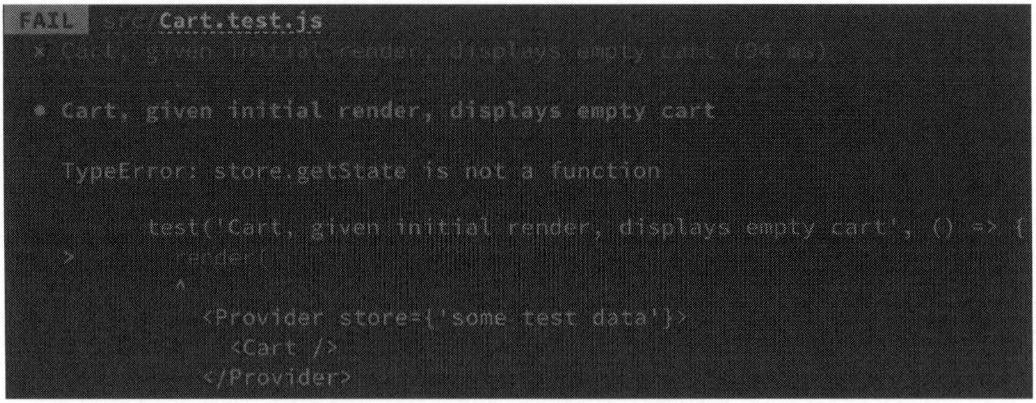

Figure 4.11 – Failed Cart Redux component test

The preceding screenshot shows the test **Cart, given initial render, displays empty cart** failed and displays `TypeError: store.getState is not a function` to the console. The ^ symbol indicates the error that occurred at the `render` method. The test failed because when the component under test renders, it tries to access a method provided by Redux to access the Redux store's state, but the method is not available. We need a way to pass all associated Redux state methods and controllable test data to the test. We will learn a strategy in the next section.

Creating a custom render method for testing Redux consuming components

In this section, we will learn how to create a custom `render` function for use in our tests. In *Chapter 1*, *Exploring React Testing Library*, we learned that React Testing Library's `render` method is used to place components in the DOM to be tested. The custom `render` method uses React Testing Library `render` method's `wrapper` option to place components into the DOM wrapped in a Redux Provider component that provides access to Redux API methods. The custom `render` method will also allow us to pass in controllable test data unique to each test. To get started, we will create a file for our method and import a number of modules:

```
import { configureStore } from '@reduxjs/toolkit'
import { render as rtlRender } from '@testing-library/react'
import faker from 'faker'
import { Provider } from 'react-redux'
import retailReducer from '../retailSlice'
```

In the previous code, we import the `configureStore` method from the Redux Toolkit library. The `configureStore` method is an abstraction over the standard Redux `createStore()` used to set up the Redux store. Next, we import the `render` method from React Testing Library and name it `rtlRender`. The `rtlRender` name is short for `React Testing Library Render`. Later in the file, we will create a custom `render` method to eliminate problems resulting from using identical method names.

Next, we import the `faker` module. We will use `faker` to automatically generate data for the initial state to pass into our component. Then, we import the `Provider` method from `React-redux` to accept and give `store` to components. Finally, we import `retailReducer` that provides methods components can use to access and modify state.

Next, we will create an object to serve as the `initialState` values for the Redux store:

```
const fakeStore = {
  retail: {
    products: [
      {
        id: faker.random.uuid(),
        title: faker.commerce.productName(),
        price: faker.commerce.price(),
        description: faker.commerce.productDescription(),
        category: faker.commerce.department(),
```

```
        image: faker.image.fashion()
      },
    ],
    cartItems: [],
    favorites: [],
    showProductDetails: null
  }
}
```

In the previous code, the variable `fakeStore` holds all initial state values for `products`, `cartItems`, `favorites`, and `showProductDetails`. The products data is an array of objects with values created by `faker`. Next, we will create a custom `render` method to use in place of React Testing Library's `render` method:

```
function render(
  ui,
  {
    initialState,
    store = configureStore({
      reducer: { retail: retailReducer },
      preloadedState: initialState
    }),
    ...renderOptions
  } = {}
) {
```

In the previous code snippet, the method accepts two arguments as parameters. First, the `ui` parameter accepts the component under test as a child to be wrapped within the custom method. The following parameter is an object with many properties. First, `initialState` accepts custom test data we can pass into our components within the test file. Next, `store` uses the `configureStore` method to set up the Redux store with `reducer` and `preloadedState`. The `reducer` property is an object that accepts `reducers` we create to manage the application state. The `preloadedState` property accepts `initialState` passed into the component in the test file. Finally, any other passed-in parameters are handled by `renderOptions`.

Next, we will create the `Wrapper` method:

```
function Wrapper({ children }) {
    return <Provider store={store}>{children}</Provider>
  }
  return rtlRender(ui, { wrapper: Wrapper, ...renderOptions })
}
```

In the preceding code, `Wrapper` accepts `children`, which will be the component under test. Next, the method returns `Provider` with `store` and `children` passed in. Finally, `render` method returns a call to `rtlRender` with `ui` and an object including the `Wrapper` method and other `renderOptions` passed in.

The last step is to export the custom code to be imported and used in test files:

```
export * from '@testing-library/react'
export { render, fakeStore }
```

In the preceding code, first, we export everything from React Testing Library. Finally, we export an object that includes the custom `render` method that overrides React Testing Library `render` method and `fakeStore` as the custom test data to use in any test. Now you know how to create a custom `render` method to use for testing Redux consuming components.

Next, we will use the custom method in a test.

Using the test Redux Provider in tests

In this section, we will use the custom `render` method to test a component. In the *Testing a context consuming Retail component* section of this chapter, we tested a `Retail` component and its child components. The development team could have decided to build the component state using Redux. The `Retail` component included `Cart` that we can test with the custom `render` method:

```
import Cart from './Cart'
import { render, screen, fakeStore } from './utils/test-utils'
```

In the previous code, first, we import the `Cart` component to test in the test file. Next, we import the `render`, `screen`, and `fakeStore` methods from our custom method file. The `render` method is the custom method created in the file. The `screen` method is the real `screen` method from React Testing Library. The `fakeStore` method is the custom test data we created in the custom method file. Next, we will write the main test code:

```
test('Cart, given initial render, displays empty cart', () => {
  render(<Cart />, { initialState: fakeStore })

  expect(screen.getByText(/0 items/i)).toBeInTheDocument()
  expect(screen.getByText(/\$0\.00/i)).toBeInTheDocument()
})
```

In the previous code, first, we use the customer `render` method to render the `Cart` component in the DOM. As a second argument to the `render` method, we pass in an object and `fakeStore` as the value to `initialState`. `fakeStore` is the default test data we can use, but we can create and pass different data specific to the test. The custom `render` method makes our code cleaner because we don't see the test code's `Provider` method. Finally, we assert that the text `0 items` and `$0.00` is in the DOM. When we run the test, we get the following output:

```
PASS  src/Cart.test.js
  ✓ Cart, given initial render, displays empty cart (34 ms)

Test Suites: 1 passed, 1 total
Tests:       1 passed, 1 total
Snapshots:   0 total
Time:        4.037 s
Ran all test suites matching /src\/Cart\.test\.js/i.
```

Figure 4.12 – Passing Cart Redux component test

The preceding screenshot shows the test **Cart, given initial render, displays empty cart** passes using the custom `render` method as expected. Please see the *Chapter 4 code samples* (https://github.com/PacktPublishing/Simplify-Testing-with-React-Testing-Library/tree/master/Chapter04/ch_04_redux) for more examples testing Redux consuming components. Now you know how to create a custom `render` method to test components that consume Redux state. The custom method can be used to test practically any Redux-consuming React component.

In the next section, we will learn how to test components that consume API data via GraphQL.

Testing components that use GraphQL

In this section, you will learn how to test components that use **GraphQL** to consume API data. In *Chapter 3, Testing Complex Components with React Testing Library*, we learned how to test components that interacted with REST APIs. The same concept to test REST API consuming components also applies with GraphQL, but with a few differences. We will use the `Table` component we tested in the *Testing integrated components* section of this chapter, only now the component will be refactored to receive data via the GraphQL server using `Apollo Client` (https://www.apollographql.com/docs/react/).

We can look at the implementation details of the `Table` component to understand how it interacts with GraphQL:

```
export const EMPLOYEES = gql`
  query GetEmployees {
    employees {
      id
      name
      department
      title
    }
  }
`
```

In the preceding code, we create an `employees` GraphQL query to access the `employees` data to render in `table` row elements within the component. The query will automatically communicate with the GraphQL server when the component renders and return `employee` data for the component to use. We will later use this query inside our test file.

The `App` component plays an important role in communicating with the GraphQL server:

```
client = new ApolloClient({
  uri: 'http://localhost:4000',
  cache: new InMemoryCache()
})

const App = () => {
  return (
    <ApolloProvider client={client}>
```

```
      <Table />
    </ApolloProvider>
  )
}
```

In the preceding code, a `client` variable is created and set to a new instance of `ApolloClient`, imported from **Apollo**. This popular library gives React components the ability to communicate with GraphQL. `ApolloClient` has a `uri` property that we can set to the URL of the running GraphQL server, which is `http://localhost:4000` in the code snippet. `ApolloClient` also sets the `cache` property to the `InMemoryCache` method.

The `InMemoryCache` method is an excellent performance-enhancing feature because it will store data received from GraphQL locally and only make additional calls to the GraphQL server when the data needs updating. The `App` component also uses `ApolloProvider` from the Apollo library to render `Table` as a child component. The `Table` component can now make queries to the GraphQL server. `ApolloProvider` behaves similarly to the Redux `Provider` component we learned about in this chapter's *Testing components that use Redux* section. Now that we understand the connection between GraphQL and the consuming `Table` component, we can start writing tests.

The first test we will write will verify that a loading message appears on the screen when `Table` initially renders:

```
import { MockedProvider } from '@apollo/client/testing'
import { act, render, screen } from '@testing-library/react'
import faker from 'faker'
import Table, { EMPLOYEES } from './Table'
```

In the preceding code, we import `MockedProvider`. `MockedProvider` is a particular method from Apollo that we can use for testing. Using `MockedProvider`, we do not need to create any custom `Provider` component as we did in the *Testing components that use Redux* section of this chapter.

Next, we import `act`, `render`, and `screen` from React Testing Library. The `act` method will let React know we are explicitly performing actions it does not expect. We will cover this in detail in the associated test. Then, we import `faker` to help generate test data. Finally, we import the `Table` component to test and the `EMPLOYEES` GraphQL query.

Next, we can create a mock GraphQL response:

```
const mocks = [
  {
    request: {
      query: EMPLOYEES
    },
    result: {
```

We create a `mocks` variable set to an array in the preceding code, with a `request` property set to our `EMPLOYEES` query. The `mocks` variable will replace the real GraphQL query with a version we can use for testing. Next, we can create the test data our test will respond with:

```
    data: {
      employees: [
        {
          id: faker.random.uuid(),
          name: faker.fake('{{name.firstName}} {{name.
            lastName}}'),
          department: faker.commerce.department(),
          title: faker.name.jobTitle()
        },
        {
          id: faker.random.uuid(),
          name: faker.fake('{{name.firstName}} {{name.
            lastName}}'),
          department: faker.commerce.department(),
          title: faker.name.jobTitle()
        }
      ]
```

In the preceding code, we create a `data` property set to an array of `employees` for the `Table` component to consume and display on the screen. The `faker` module is used to eliminate the need to create hardcoded values. Now we can write the main test code:

```
test('given initial render, returns loading message', () => {
  render(
    <MockedProvider mocks={mocks}>
```

```
        <Table />
      </MockedProvider>
    )
    expect(screen.getByText(/Loading.../)).toBeInTheDocument()
})
```

In the previous code, we render the `Table` component inside `MockedProvider` with passed-in `mocks` data. Then, we assert that the text **Loading...** is in the DOM. The loading text is the first thing to display when the component renders until the frontend React application receives data from the GraphQL server.

For the next test, we will verify the `completed` state is achieved, meaning the component has received and rendered employee data:

```
test('given completed state, renders employee data', async ()
  => {
  render(
    <MockedProvider mocks={mocks}>
      <Table />
    </MockedProvider>
  )
    await act(() => new Promise(resolve =>
      setTimeout(resolve, 0)))
  screen.debug()
  expect(screen.getAllByTestId('row').length).toEqual(2)
})
```

In the previous code, we render the `Table` component inside `MockedProvider` with passed-in `mocks` data. Then, we set `Promise` to the `resolved` state wrapped in the `act` method. Although we are not accessing the real GraphQL server, the Apollo methods we use are asynchronous and take some time to complete. We explicitly complete the asynchronous process after `0` seconds to continue the test steps.

The 0 second value may seem odd to force the `resolved` state but is necessary because asynchronous JavaScript actions will wait for some time before completion and continuing with the following action. If we do not use the `act` method, our test will pass but also render an error message to the screen:

```
Warning: An update to Table inside a test was not wrapped in act(...).
When testing, code that causes React state updates should be wrapped into act(...):
```

Figure 4.13 – Not wrapped in act error

The preceding screenshot shows the error message displayed in the console when we do not use the `act` method to handle explicit component updates that React does not know about. Finally, we assert that two `row` elements are found in the DOM.

For the last test, we will verify that the error state results in the error message being displayed on the screen:

```
test('given error state, renders error message', async () =>
  {
    const mocks = [{ request: { query: EMPLOYEES }, error: new
      Error() }]

    render(
      <MockedProvider mocks={mocks}>
        <Table />
      </MockedProvider>
    )
    await act(() => new Promise(resolve => setTimeout(resolve,
      0)))
    expect(screen.getByText(/Error/i)).toBeInTheDocument()
})
```

In the previous code, we render the `Table` component inside `MockedProvider` with passed-in `mocks` data. However, unlike previous tests, we set the `error` property to a new instance of the `Error` object. When the `error` property is set, it means that something happened, preventing the process of sending and receiving data from the GraphQL server to the frontend.

Next, we set `Promise` to the `resolved` state wrapped in the `act` method as we did in the previous test. Finally, we assert that the text `Error` is in the document. When we run the tests, we get the following output:

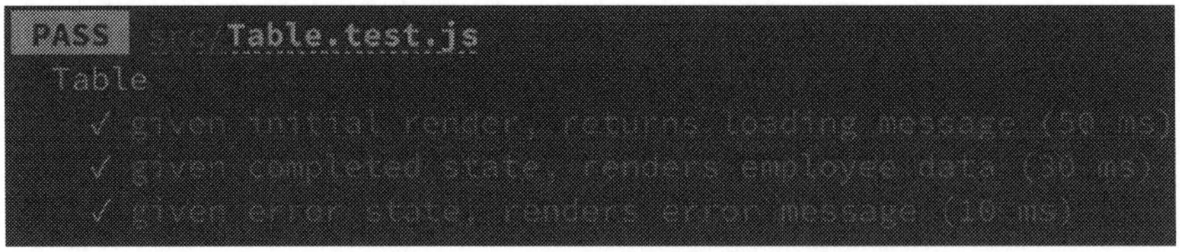

Figure 4.14 – Table component test results

Now you know how to test components that consume GraphQL server data using Apollo Client. As GraphQL continues to gain popularity, it will be helpful to have the testing strategies we covered in your toolbox to verify expected behavior quickly.

In the next section, we will learn how to test components that use the popular Material-UI component library for frontend development.

Testing Components that use Material-UI

In this section, we will learn how to test components that use the Material-UI component library. You can select DOM elements rendered by Material-UI components out of the box with React Testing Library in most cases. However, sometimes it is helpful to add component properties that render as attributes on resulting DOM elements. We will learn how to add properties to test the `Vote` and `Customer Table` components.

Adding an ARIA label to test a Vote component

In the *Testing a context consuming Vote component* section of this chapter, we tested a `Vote` component.

We could use components from Material-UI to rebuild the component:

```
<div>
    <Box display="flex" flexDirection="column" css={{ width:
      100 }}>
    <Button
        onClick={() => voteLike()}
        disabled={hasVotedLike}
        variant="contained"
        color="primary"
```

```
            >
                <ThumbUpIcon />
            </Button>
```

In the previous code, we used the `Box`, `Button`, and `ThumbUpIcon` components from Material-UI to quickly build the **thumbs up** button complete with **Cascading Style Sheet (CSS)** styles already included to make the button look nice.

Next, we will build the remaining parts of the component:

```
            <Typography variant="h3" align="center">
                {totalLikes}
            </Typography>
            <Button
                onClick={() => voteDislike()}
                disabled={hasVotedDislike}
                variant="contained"
                color="primary"
            >
                <ThumbDownAltIcon />
            </Button>
        </Box>
    </div>
```

In the preceding code, we use the `Typography`, `Button`, and `ThumbDownAltIcon` components from Material-UI to build the thumbs down button and display the total likes number on the screen. When we render the component in the browser, we get the following output:

Figure 4.15 – Material-UI Vote component

The preceding screenshot shows a **thumbs up** and **thumbs down** button and the number **10** representing the current number of likes. Like the `Vote` component we tested in previous sections of this chapter, a user can vote up or down to change the total likes. However, grabbing and clicking the buttons with React Testing Library would be difficult with the current component implementation. There are no accessible ways to access the buttons, such as a label.

To solve this problem, we can add `aria-label` properties to the `Button` components. `aria-label` will add a visible label to elements allowing users with screen readers to understand the elements' purpose. We can add `aria-label` to the component like so:

```
<Button
  aria-label="thumbs up"
```

We added **thumbs up** `aria-label` to the first `Button` component in the previous code snippet. Next, we will add `aria-label` to the other `Button` component:

```
<Button
  aria-label="thumbs down"
```

In the previous code, we added **thumbs down** `aria-label` to the second `Button` component. Material UI will forward the `Button` `aria-label` properties to the resulting button element that will render in the DOM. Since `aria-label` attributes are accessible by all users, including those using assistive devices to navigate the screen, React Testing Library can grab elements by those attributes. Now that we can select the elements, we can write tests and assert the resulting behavior.

For the first test, we will verify that a user can only decrease the total like count by one:

```
test('given multiple "down" votes, total likes only decrease
    by one', () => {
  render(<Vote totalGlobalLikes={10} />)
  const thumbsUpBtn = screen.getByRole('button', { name: /
    thumbs up/i })

  user.click(thumbsUpBtn)
  user.click(thumbsUpBtn)
  user.click(thumbsUpBtn)

  expect(screen.getByText(/11/i)).toBeInTheDocument()
})
```

In the previous code, we render the `Vote` component with the value of `10` for `totalGlobalLikes`. Next, we grab the **thumbs up** button by its name provided via the `aria-label` attribute we added and assign it to the `thumbsUpBtn` variable. Next, we click the **thumbs up** button three times and finally assert that the value `11` is in the DOM.

For the next test, we will verify that a user can remove their **"up"** vote:

```
test('given retracted "up" vote, returns original total
    likes', () => {
  render(<Vote totalGlobalLikes={10} />)

  const thumbsUpBtn = screen.getByRole('button', { name: /
      thumbs up/i })
  const thumbsDownBtn = screen.getByRole('button', { name: /
      thumbs down/i })

  user.click(thumbsUpBtn)
  user.click(thumbsDownBtn)

  expect(screen.getByText(/10/i)).toBeInTheDocument()
})
```

In the previous code, we render the Vote component with the value of 10 for totalGlobalLikes. Next, we grab the **thumbs up** and **thumbs down** buttons by their name attribute provided via the aria-label properties we added to both Buttons and assign them to variables.

Next, we click the **thumbs up** and **thumbs down** buttons and finally assert that the value 10 is on the screen. When we run the test, we get the following results:

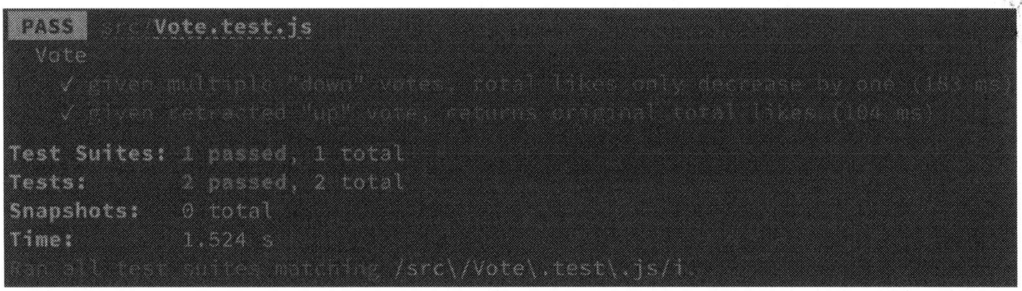

Figure 4.16 – Material-UI Vote test results

The previous screenshot shows that the tests **given multiple "down" votes, total likes only decrease by one**, and **given retracted "up" vote, returns original total likes** pass as expected.

As a challenge, try writing tests for the following scenarios: **given "up" vote, total likes increases by one; given multiple "up" votes, total likes only increase by one;** and **given retracted "down" vote, returns original total likes**. The solutions for these test scenarios can be found in the *chapter 4 code samples*. Now you know how to make Material-UI components testable by adding aria-labels.

In the next section, we will learn how to add an attribute specific to React Testing Library to make components testable.

Adding a test ID to test a CustomerTable component

In the previous section, we learned how to make Material-UI components testable by adding `aria-labels`. In this section, we will learn how to add `data-testid` to make components testable. `data-testid` is another option to query DOM elements with React Testing Library. The `data-testid` query is a last-resort way to grab DOM elements when other preferred methods such as `*byText` or `*byRole` cannot be used, and we want to avoid using `class` or `ID` selectors. We can use `data-testid` by attaching it as an attribute to a DOM element:

```
<h5 data-testid="product-type">Electronics</h5>
```

We add a `"product-type"` `data-testid` to select the heading element uniquely in the previous code snippet. We will test a `CustomerTable` component in this section that accepts customer data and renders the following to the screen:

filter results				
Name	Avatar	**Address**	email	phone
Darcee Staveley		691 Bashford Street	dstaveley0@angelfire.com	(330) 7511940
Valli Port		58 Wayridge Hill	vport1@istockphoto.com	(807) 5590500
Joete Oolahan	176 × 102	18 Bashford Trail	joolahan2@flavors.me	(670) 3201530
Stephanus Grane		729 Fuller Pass	sgrane3@dailymail.co.uk	(410) 8723323
Margery Purdy		519 Anhalt Lane	mpurdy4@technorati.com	(498) 6639434

Figure 4.17 – Material-UI table component

The previous screenshot shows a table with multiple rows of customer data. A user can use the **filter results** input to narrow the output to specific rows. For example, if a customer searches the text da, the following results will be displayed:

filter results				
da|				

Name	Avatar	Address	email	phone
Darcee Staveley	●	691 Bashford Street	dstaveley0@angelfire.com	(330) 7511940
Stephanus Grane	○	729 Fuller Pass	sgrane3@dailymail.co.uk	(410) 8723323

Figure 4.18 – Material-UI table filtered results

The preceding screenshot shows two resulting rows. The two rows are displayed as matching results because the text **da** is visible in the rows' associated columns. We will write three tests for the component.

For the first test, we will verify that the component can receive and render passed-in customer data:

```
const fakeCustomers = [
  {
    id: 1,
    name: 'John Doe',
    email: 'john@mail.com',
    address: '123 John Street',
    phone: '(111) 1111111',
    avatar: 'http://dummyimage.com/235x233.jpg/ff4444/ffffff'
  },
  // two additional objects
]
```

In the preceding code, we create an array of test objects to pass into the component. It should be noted that the code snippet only shows one customer object. The code sample for the CustomerTable test file will have three.

Next, we can write the main test code:

```
test('given data, renders table rows', () => {
    render(<CustomerTable data={fakeCustomers} />)

    expect(screen.getAllByTestId('row').length).toEqual(3)
})
```

In the previous code, first, we render `CustomerTable` with `fakeCustomers` passed into the `data` property. Finally, we assert that the number of rows is equal to 3. We use the `getAllByTestId` query to access all the rows. The `*allBy` queries allow us to grab multiple, similar DOM elements. In the code implementation for `CustomerTable`, `data-testid` is added as a property to each `TableRow` component created for each customer data object:

```
<TableRow data-testid="row" key={customer.id}>
```

In the previous code, a `data-testid` property is added to the `TableRow` component. The `data-testid` is used because the preferred query methods cannot be used to select all the rows in this scenario. For the second test, we verify that queries returning one match return one result:

```
test('given single-matching query, single result returned',
() => {
    render(<CustomerTable data={testData} />)
    const searchBox = screen.getByRole('textbox')

    user.type(searchBox, 'john')
    expect(screen.queryAllByTestId('row').length).toEqual(1)
})
```

In the previous code, first, we render `CustomerTable` with `testData` passed into the `data` property. Then, we grab the textbox and store it in the `searchBox` variable. Finally, we assert that the number of rows in the DOM is 1.

For the final test, we will verify that non-matching queries return no `row` elements to the screen:

```
test('given non-matching query, no results returned', () => {
    render(<CustomerTable data={testData} />)
    const searchBox = screen.getByRole('textbox')
```

```
    user.type(searchBox, 'zzz')
    expect(screen.queryAllByTestId('row').length).toEqual(0)
  })
```

The preceding code is similar to the previous test with two differences. First, we type `zzz` into `searchBox`. Then, we assert that `0  row` elements are found in the DOM. When we run the tests, we get the following output:

```
PASS    src/CustomerTable.test.js
  CustomerTable
    ✓ given data, renders table rows (121 ms)
    ✓ given single-matching query, single result returned (170 ms)
    ✓ given non-matching query, no results returned (89 ms)

Test Suites: 1 passed, 1 total
Tests:       3 passed, 3 total
Snapshots:   0 total
Time:        4.998 s
Ran all test suites matching /src\/CustomerTable\.test\.js/i.
```

Figure 4.19 – Material-UI table test results

The previous screenshot shows that the tests **given data, renders table rows**, **given single-matching query, single result returned**, and **given non-matching query, no results returned** all pass as expected. As a challenge, try writing a test for the scenario **given multi-matching query, multiple results returned**. The previous test scenario solution can be found in the *Chapter 4 code samples* (`https://github.com/PacktPublishing/Simplify-Testing-with-React-Testing-Library/tree/master/Chapter04/ch_04_mui`).

This section's content has provided you with the skills to test specific Material-UI components by adding `aria-label` and `data-testid` attributes to grab them with React Testing Library when needed.

Summary

In this chapter, you have learned how to test components using the integration test approach compared to the unit test approach with mocked dependencies. You know how to test components that use the Context API to manage application state. You also learned how to create a custom method to test components in projects using the third-party Redux library. Finally, you learned how to add attributes to test components built using the popular Material-UI library.

In the next chapter, we will learn how to refactor tests for legacy projects.

Questions

1. Explain the benefits of testing integrated components versus in isolation.
2. When should you use the `data-testid` attribute to grab components?
3. When should you use the `act` method from React Testing Library?

5

Refactoring Legacy Applications with React Testing Library

In the previous chapter, we learned how to test components in isolation separate from dependencies. We learned how the benefits of testing components can be integrated with other components. We also learned how to test components that use popular third-party **User Interface** (**UI**) and state management tools. By the end of this chapter, you will learn strategies for dealing with breaking changes while refactoring legacy React applications. You will learn how to update production packages while using React Testing Library tests to guide you in resolving breaking changes. You will also learn how to convert tests written in Enzyme or ReactTestUtils to React Testing Library.

In this chapter, we're going to cover the following main topics:

- Using tests to catch regressions when updating dependencies
- Refactoring tests written with Enzyme

- Refactoring tests written with ReactTestUtils
- Refactoring tests to comply with common testing best practices

The skills acquired in this chapter will enable you to reduce the burden of refactoring legacy applications.

Technical requirements

For the examples in this chapter, you will need to have Node.js installed on your machine. We will be using the `create-react-app` CLI tool for all code examples. Please familiarize yourself with the tool if required before starting the chapter. Also, a basic understanding of the Material UI library will be helpful.

Code snippets will be provided throughout the chapter to help you understand the code under test, but the objective is understanding how to test the code. You can find the code examples for this chapter here: `https://github.com/PacktPublishing/Simplify-Testing-with-React-Testing-Library/tree/master/Chapter05`.

Using tests to catch regressions when updating dependencies

In this section, we will learn how to use tests to drive the updating of application dependencies. The tests will help verify that the application code continues to work as expected and allow us to quickly catch regressions if they occur after updating dependencies. The budgeting application renders the following when the application is running:

Figure 5.1 – Budget application

The preceding screenshot shows a summary section that includes **Income**, **Spending**, and **Left over** amounts based on user input. A user can click the **SET INCOME** button to update the value for **Income**:

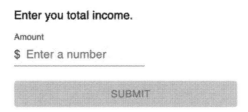

Figure 5.2 – Setting the budget income

The preceding screenshot shows a model that allows the user to enter and submit a number to update the value for **Income**. A user can also create budgets for various categories:

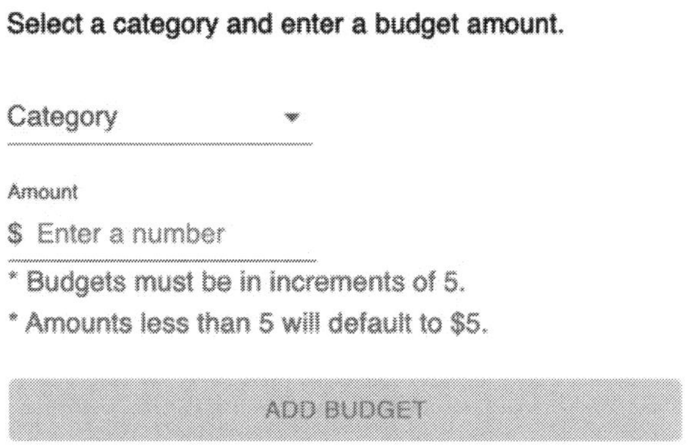

Select a category and enter a budget amount.

Category ▼

Amount

$ Enter a number

* Budgets must be in increments of 5.

* Amounts less than 5 will default to $5.

ADD BUDGET

Figure 5.3 – Adding a budget category

The preceding screenshot shows a model that allows the user to select **Category** and **Amount** and add the new budget. The model also displays a message informing the user of acceptable values for the budget. Once the user creates a new budget, the budget is added to the screen:

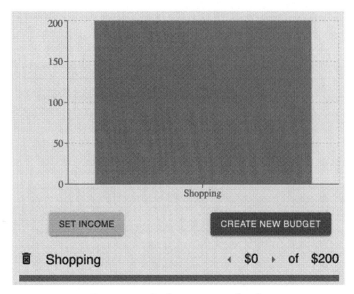

Figure 5.4 – Budget category details

The preceding screenshot shows a **Shopping** budget of **$200** added to the screen. An associated bar graph and a spending progress bar are added to the budget. A user can click the triangle buttons to add amounts to the budget or click the trashcan icon to delete the budget.

The budgeting application has the following production dependencies:

```
"dependencies": {
    "@material-ui/core": "^1.4.2",
    "@material-ui/icons": "^2.0.1",
    "react": "^16.4.2",
    "react-dom": "^16.4.2",
    "recharts": "^1.1.0",
    "uuid": "^3.3.2"
},
```

The preceding code shows the current versions of all project dependencies. We will update "@material-ui/core" to version "4.11.3", "@material-ui/icons" to version "4.11.2", and "recharts" to version "2.0.4", so the application has up-to-date dependency code. The approach we will use to update the dependencies will involve having a suite of automated tests running to help catch any regressions after each dependency is updated. The budgeting application does not have any existing tests.

In situations where a legacy application has no existing tests, a great way to get started is by writing automated UI end-to-end tests for critical workflows before adding tests at other test levels. Please refer to *Chapter 7, End-to-End UI Testing with Cypress*, for related content.

This chapter will teach you how to write automated component tests with React Testing Library before starting the dependency refactor task. Please see *Chapter 2, Working with React Testing Library*, for installation instructions. Now that you have learned about the application and the approach to updating dependencies, we will get down to writing regression tests in the next section.

Creating the regression test suite

In this section, we will write several integration tests with React Testing Library to add confidence that we can catch regressions while updating application dependencies. Please refer to *Chapter 4, Integration Testing and Third-Party Libraries in Your Application*, for content related to writing integration testing. We will write tests for the following major functionalities: setting the income, deleting a budget, creating a budget, and budget details. For the first test, we will target the *setting the income* functionality by verifying that a user can enter an amount for income:

```
function setOneDollarIncome() {
    user.click(screen.getByText(/set income/i));
    user.type(screen.getByRole('spinbutton'), '1');
    user.click(screen.getByText(/submit/i));
}
```

In the previous code, we create a function, `setOneDollarIncome`, to set an income amount of *$1*. The `setOneDollarIncome` function will reduce repetitive code in successive tests. Next, we will write the main test code:

```
test('SetIncome, given income amount, sets income', () => {
  render(<App />);

  setOneDollarIncome();
  const leftOverBudget = screen.getByText(/left over:/i);
  const leftOverBudgetAmount = within(leftOverBudget).
    getByText(/\$1/i);

  expect(leftOverBudgetAmount).toBeInTheDocument();
  expect(
    screen.getByRole('heading', { name: /income: \$1/i })
  ).toBeInTheDocument();
});
```

In the preceding code, first, we render the App component in the DOM. Next, we set an income amount of *$1* via the `setOneDollarIncome` function. Next, we grab the `left over` text and use the `within` method from React Testing Library to access the dollar amount text. The `within` method can be used in situations where we want to access the child elements of a parent element. When we run the application, the resulting HTML element output for the **Left Over** section on the screen is as follows:

```
<p class="MuiTypography-root BudgetSummary-leftoverText-4
  MuiTypography-body1">
  Left over: <span class="BudgetSummary-profit-6">$1</span>
</p>
```

In the preceding code, a p element has the text `Left over` as child content. In the test code, we grab the p element via the `Left Over` text and store it in the `leftOverBudget` variable. Then, we use `within` to grab the span element with the text $1 and store it in the `leftOverBudgetAmount` variable.

Finally, we assert that `leftOverBudgetAmount` is in the DOM. For the next test, we will target the *creating a budget* functionality by verifying the resulting amount in the *Budget Summary* section once a user sets a budget:

```
function createCarBudget(amount = '5') {
  user.click(screen.getByText(/create new budget/i));
```

```
  user.selectOptions(screen.getByRole('combobox', { name: /
    category/i }), [
    screen.getByText('Auto'),
  ]);
  user.type(screen.getByRole('spinbutton'), amount);
  user.click(screen.getByText(/add budget/i));
}
```

In the previous code, we create a function, `createCarBudget`, to reduce the repetitive steps of creating a budget that will be used in multiple test cases. A default value of 5 will be used if no value for the `amount` parameter is passed as an argument to the function. Next, we will write the main test code:

```
test.each`
  budgetAmount | spending           | leftOver
  ${'4'}       | ${'Spending: $5'}  | ${'$-4'}
  ${'5'}       | ${'Spending: $5'}  | ${'$-4'}
  ${'6'}       | ${'Spending: $10'} | ${'$-9'}
`(
  'given budget, updates budget summary',
  ({ budgetAmount, spending, leftOver }) => {
```

In the preceding code, we use the `each` method from Jest to allow the same test to be run multiple times with different values. The `budgetAmount`, `spending`, and `leftOver` variables represent the test's values for each test iteration. We have three rows of data under the variables to pass into the variables for each of the three test runs. Next, we arrange and perform actions in the test:

```
    render(<App />);
    setOneDollarIncome();


    createCarBudget(budgetAmount);
    const leftOverBudget = screen.getByText(/left over:/i);
    const leftOverBudgetAmount = within(leftOverBudget).
      getByText(leftOver);
```

In the preceding code, first we render the app in the DOM and invoke the
`setOneDollarIncome` function. Next, we invoke the `createCarBudget` function
and pass in the value of `budgetAmount` for the current test iteration. Next, we
grab the element associated with the **Left Over Budget** section and assign it to the
`leftOverBudget` variable, similar to what we did in the previous test. Finally, we make
the following assertions:

```
expect(leftOverBudgetAmount).toBeInTheDocument();
expect(
    screen.getByRole('heading', { name: spending })
).toBeInTheDocument();
}
);
```

In the previous code, first, we assert that `leftOverBudgetAmount` is in the DOM.
Finally, we assert that the heading element for the current value of `name` is in the DOM.
By way of a challenge, write a test that verifies that a budget chart is displayed for a created
budget.

The solution for the previous scenario can be found in the code samples for *Chapter 5,
Refactoring Legacy Applications with React Testing Library*.

For the next test, we will target the *deleting a budget* functionality by verifying that a
deleted budget has been removed from the screen:

```
test('DeleteBudget, given deleted budget, budget removed from
    DOM', () => {
  render(<App />);
  setOneDollarIncome();
  createCarBudget();

  user.click(screen.getByLabelText(/trash can/i));

  expect(screen.queryByRole('listitem')).not.
      toBeInTheDocument();
});
```

In the preceding code, first, we arrange our test by rendering the App component in the DOM and invoking the setOneDollarIncome and createCarBudget functions. Next, we click the trash can icon. Finally, we assert that no listitem elements are in the DOM.

Since the listitem elements render the budgets on the screen, we can be confident that the functionality works as expected if none are found in the DOM. For the last test, we will target the *budget details* functionality by verifying that adding expenses updates the budget's progress:

```
test('given budget expense, updates budget progress', async
    () => {
  render(<App />);
  setOneDollarIncome();
  createCarBudget();

  user.click(screen.getByRole('button', { name: /
      arrowright/i }));

  expect(
    screen.getByRole('heading', { name: /\$5 of \$5/i })
  ).toBeInTheDocument();
});
```

In the preceding code, first, we arrange our test by rendering the App component in the DOM and invoking the setOneDollarIncome and createCarBudget functions similar to the previous test. Next, we click the right arrow icon. Finally, we assert that the text, $5 of $5, is present on the screen.

As a challenge, try to write the code for the following test scenario: Budget, given budget, displays details. The solutions for this test scenario can be found in the code samples for *Chapter 5, Refactoring Legacy Applications with React Testing Library*.

When we run our tests, we receive the following output:

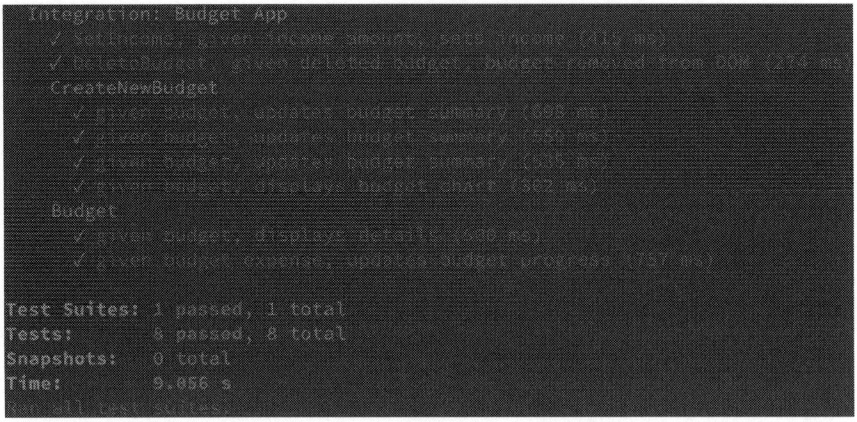

Figure 5.5 – Budget app test results

The preceding screenshot shows that all the tests pass. Now that we have a passing regression test suite, we will upgrade the production dependencies for the application in the next section. It should be noted that our tests are automatically set up to run in **watch mode**, a Jest feature that automatically re-runs tests any time an associated component file is changed.

The watch mode feature provides you with confidence that we can quickly discover regressions as code changes are implemented. For projects not automatically set up to run Jest in watch mode, simply pass the `--watch` flag when you execute Jest from the command line.

Upgrading the Material UI dependencies

In the previous section, we created a regression test suite. In this section, we will delete all highlighted text and get the latest dependency code by upgrading the `@material-ui/icons` and `@material-ui/core` dependencies. The `@material-ui/icons` package depends on `@material-ui/core`, so we will update both dependencies simultaneously.

Inside the `package.json` file, replace the current version of `@material-ui/icons` 2.0.1 with 4.11.2, `@material-ui/core` with 4.11.3, and reinstall all dependencies. Now, when we run our tests, we receive the following output:

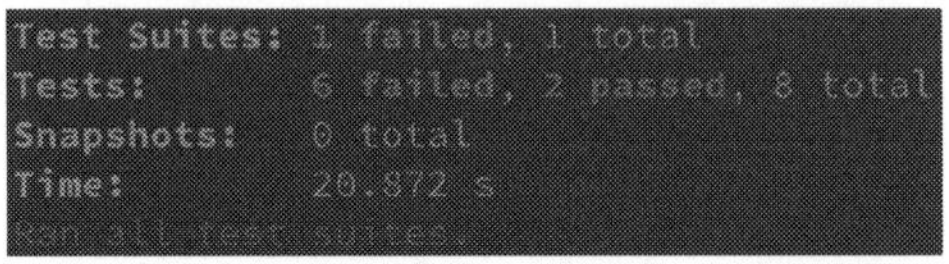

Figure 5.6 – Budget app failed test results

In the previous screenshot, the test results indicate that the dependency updates broke our tests. The results provide detailed information related to why each test failed. The following is a high-level version of the test results information displayed in the console:

```
Integration: Budget App > SetIncome, given income amount, sets
income
      TestingLibraryElementError: Unable to find an accessible
         element with the role "heading" and name `/income: \$1/i`
Integration: Budget App > Budget > given budget, displays
details
      TestingLibraryElementError: Unable to find an accessible
         element with the role "heading" and name `/\$0 of \$5/i`
Integration: Budget App > Budget > given budget expense,
updates budget progress
      TestingLibraryElementError: Unable to find an accessible
         element with the role "heading" and name `/\$5 of \$5/i`
Integration: Budget App > CreateNewBudget > given budget,
updates budget summary
      TestingLibraryElementError: Unable to find an accessible
         element with the role "heading" and name "Spending: $10"
      TestingLibraryElementError: Unable to find an accessible
         element with the role "heading" and name "Spending: $5"
```

In the previous console output, the test results inform us of specific tests that failed due to not being able to find targeted heading elements in the DOM. When we updated the dependencies, a regression occurred in our source code. Error messages are also displayed in the console, providing information to pinpoint the problems in the source code. The following is a high-level version of the error messages displayed in the console:

```
Warning: Failed prop type: Invalid prop `spacing` of value
`24` supplied to `ForwardRef(Grid)`, expected one of
[0,1,2,3,4,5,6,7,8,9,10].
Warning: Failed prop type: Invalid prop `variant` of value
`title` supplied to `ForwardRef(Typography)`, expected one of
["h1","h2","h3","h4","h5","h6","subtitle1","subtitle2","body1",
"body2","caption","button","overline","srOnly","inherit"].
Warning: Failed prop type: Invalid prop `variant` of value
`subheading` supplied to `ForwardRef(Typography)`, expected
one of ["h1","h2","h3","h4","h5","h6","subtitle1","subtitle2",
"body1","body2","caption","button","overline","srOnly",
"inherit"].
```

```
Material-UI: theme.spacing.unit usage has been deprecated.
It will be removed in v5.
You can replace `theme.spacing.unit * y` with `theme.
spacing(y)`.
```

The error messages inform us that our source code is now using outdated property values from the material UI dependencies in the previous console output, which resulted in our tests not finding specific `heading` elements and failing. The error message output also tells us in which individual component file the error occurred under each error message. For example, the source of the error, `Material-UI: theme.spacing.unit usage has been deprecated.`, can be found here:

```
(src/components/SetIncome.js:27:26)
```

The preceding console output informs us that the error source is on space 26 of line 27 of the `SetIncome` component file. Now that we know the specifics of why each test failed, we can update the source code appropriately.

We will keep our tests running in watch mode while updating the source code to add confidence we will catch any new regressions that may occur due to updating the code. Once we update the code in our component files based on the error messages, we receive the following output when we run our tests:

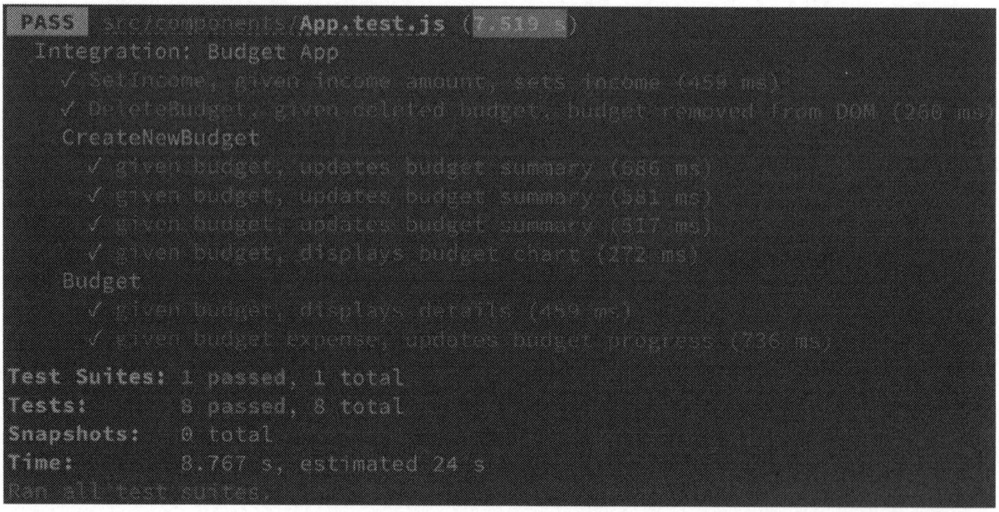

Figure 5.7 – Budget app updated dependency test results

The preceding screenshot shows that all tests are now passing after updating the source code based on the error messages. Now you know how to update production dependencies and add tests to legacy applications. The great thing about using React Testing Library during this task is knowing that we never need to update our test code while we update the source code.

Our test code does not depend on the components' implementation details, we are free to change the source code however necessary as long as the resulting DOM output and behavior do not change. In the next section, we will learn how to refactor tests for legacy code that uses Enzyme.

Refactoring tests written with Enzyme

In the previous section, we learned how to update production dependencies and add component tests to legacy applications. In this section, we will learn how to replace existing legacy tests written in **Enzyme** with React Testing Library. Before React Testing Library was created, Enzyme was a popular library to test the UI of React components. Enzyme is a great tool, but the design of the API allows the implementation details of components to be tested, resulting in developers having to update test code frequently as they update their source code. We will replace legacy Enzyme tests with React Testing Library to resolve the problem of having to update tests that focus on implementation details continually.

We will use this approach to refactor legacy Enzyme tests to keep the current tests while installing and incrementally refactoring them with React Testing Library. Please refer to *Chapter 2, Working with React Testing Library*, for installation instructions. Once we are finished refactoring the legacy code and all tests are passing, we will remove Enzyme from the application. The tests will be refactored to tests created in the *Creating the regression test suite* section of this chapter. The first test we will refactor verifies that a user can set an income amount:

```
test('SetIncome, given income amount, sets income', () => {
    const wrapper = mount(<App />);

    wrapper.find('SetIncome').props().setIncome(1);

    expect(wrapper.find('h3#income').text()).toEqual('Income:
        $1');
});
```

In the preceding code, the `mount` method from Enzyme is used to render the `App` component in the DOM. Next, the `find` method is used to locate the `SetIncome` component and invoke the `setIncome` method with the value 1. Finally, an assertion is made to verify that the text value of the `h3` element with the `id` of `income` equals `Income: $1`.

There are many implementation details that would break the test if changed. For example, if the names of the `SetIncome` component or the `setIncome` method are changed, the test would break. A change to `income id` would also break the test. We can refactor the test to focus on the user's perspective like so:

```
test('SetIncome, given income amount, sets income', () => {
    render(<App />);

    setOneDollarIncome();
    const leftOverBudget = screen.getByText(/left over:/i);
    const leftOverBudgetAmount = within(leftOverBudget).
      getByText(/\$1/i);

    expect(leftOverBudgetAmount).toBeInTheDocument();
```

In the preceding code, we refactored the Enzyme test code that verifies that a user can set an income amount with React Testing Library. The next test that we will refactor verifies that the *Budget summary* section is updated when a user creates a budget:

```
test('given budget, updates budget summary', () => {
    const wrapper = mount(<App />);
    const budgetAmount = Math.ceil(parseInt(5, 10) / 5) *
5;

    wrapper.find('CreateNewBudget').props().addNewBudget({
        id: '1',
        category: 'Auto',
        amount: budgetAmount,
        amtSpent: 0,
    });
    wrapper.find('CreateNewBudget').props().
      setTotalSpending(budgetAmount);
```

In the preceding code, first we render the App component in the DOM. Next, we use the ceil method from the Math object and the parseInt method to round the passed-in budget amount of 5 to the nearest multiple of 5. Next, we use the find method to call the addNewBudget method inside the CreateNewBudget component with an object representing the budget.

Then, we call the setTotalSpending method in the same component with the result of the budgetAmount variable. Next, we will make assertions:

```
expect(wrapper.find('h3#spending').text()).toEqual('Spending:
  $5');
expect(wrapper.find('span#leftover').text()).toEqual("$-5");
```

In the previous code, we assert that the text value of the h3 element with the id of spending is equal to Spending: $5. Finally, we assert that the text value of the span element with the id of leftover is equal to $-5. We can refactor the previous code with React Testing Library like so:

```
test('given budget, updates budget summary', () => {
  render(<App />);
  setOneDollarIncome();

  createCarBudget(5);
  const leftOverBudget = screen.getByText(/left over:/i);
  const leftOverBudgetAmount = within(leftOverBudget).
    getByText('df');

  expect(leftOverBudgetAmount).toBeInTheDocument();
  expect(screen.getByRole('heading', { name: 'Spending: $5'
}))).toBeInTheDocument();
});
```

In the preceding code, we refactored the Enzyme test code that verifies that the *Budget summary* section is updated when a user creates a budget with React Testing Library. The next test that we will refactor verifies that a chart is displayed when a user creates a budget:

```
test('given budget, displays budget chart', () => {
  const wrapper = mount(<App />);
  const budgetAmount = Math.ceil(parseInt(5, 10) / 5) * 5;
```

```
        wrapper.find('CreateNewBudget').props().addNewBudget({
          id: '1',
          category: 'Auto',
          amount: budgetAmount,
          amtSpent: 0,
        });
        wrapper.find('CreateNewBudget').props().
          setTotalSpending(budgetAmount);
        wrapper.update();
```

In the preceding code, we render the App component in the DOM using the mount method and create a budgetAmount variable to convert the budget into a multiple of five similar to the previous test. Next. We use the find method to call the addNewBudget method inside the CreateNewBudget component and pass in a budget object.

Then, we call the setTotalSpending method inside CreateNewBudget and pass in the budget amount. Next, we call the update method to sync our test with the code created by the Chart component. Next, we can make assertions:

```
        expect(wrapper.find('div#chart')).toBeTruthy();
      });
```

In the preceding code, we assert that the div element with the id of chart is truthy, meaning it was found in the DOM. As we saw in the *Creating the regression test suite* section of this chapter, all the test cases for the budget application written in React Testing Library will pass as expected when run.

Now that all the Enzyme tests have been refactored to React Testing Library, we can remove the enzyme and enzyme-adapter-react-16 dependencies from the package.json file. We can also remove the following code from the setupTests. js file:

```
import Enzyme from 'enzyme';
import Adapter from 'enzyme-adapter-react-16';


Enzyme.configure({ adapter: new Adapter() });
```

The preceding code is used to configure Enzyme to work in the test files. The code is no longer needed after removing Enzyme from the application. Now you know how to refactor legacy tests created with Enzyme to React Testing Library. The React Testing Library tests provide greater confidence and reduce the chances of tests breaking when we refactor the source code.

In the next section, we will learn how to refactor tests created with `ReactTestUtils`.

Refactoring tests written with **ReactTestUtils**

In the previous section, we learned how to convert tests written in Enzyme to React Testing Library. The process involved refactoring existing tests and then uninstalling the Enzyme library. In this section, we will use a similar process, only we will not have to uninstall an existing testing library. The `ReactTestUtils` module is included with React, so we can simply not import the module in our test file when we don't want to use it. Since the refactoring process is similar to the previous section, we will only look at one example in this section. The test we will refactor verifies that a user can set an income amount:

```
import React from 'react';
import ReactDOM from 'react-dom';
import { act } from 'react-dom/test-utils';
import App from './App';
```

In the preceding code, we import `React`, `ReactDOM`, and the `act` method. The `act` method imported from the `test-utils` module is used to sync component updates and ensure that our tests behave in ways similar to how React does in the browser. Next, we will arrange the code needed for the test:

```
it('SetIncome, given initial render, displays budget summary
    values', () => {
  let container = document.createElement('div');
  document.body.appendChild(container);


  act(() => {
    ReactDOM.render(<App />, container);
  });
```

In the preceding code, we create a `div` element to render in the DOM and assign it to the `container` variable. Next, we attach the `container` variable to the `body` element of the DOM. Then, we render the `App` component in `container`, wrapped in the `act` method. Next, we will grab DOM elements and assert on their text values:

```
const income = container.querySelector('h3#income');
const spending = container.querySelector('#spending');
const leftover = container.querySelector('#leftover');

expect(income.textContent).toBe('Income: $0');
expect(spending.textContent).toBe('Spending: $0');
expect(leftover.textContent).toBe('$0');
```

In the preceding code, we use the `querySelector` method to access the `income`, `spending`, and `leftover` elements in the DOM. Then, we assert the values of the previous three elements using the `textContent` property. Finally, we will add code to clean up the test:

```
document.body.removeChild(container);
```

In the preceding code, we remove the container element from the DOM. Removing the container will ensure that we can start successive tests from a clean slate. We can refactor the previous test using React Testing Library:

```
it('SetIncome, given initial render, displays budget summary
  values', () => {
  render(<App />);

  const income = screen.getByRole('heading', { name: /income:
    \$0/i });
  const spending = screen.getByRole('heading', { name: /
    spending: \$0/i });
  const leftover = screen.getByText(/left over:/i);

  expect(income).toHaveTextContent('Income: $0');
  expect(spending).toHaveTextContent('Spending: $0');
  expect(leftover).toHaveTextContent('$0');
});
```

In the preceding code, we refactored the `SetIncome, given initial render, displays budget summary values` test using React Testing Library. The React Testing Library version of the test is cleaner and is more resilient to source code changes because it does not select DOM elements using implementation details. When we run the test, we get the following output:

Figure 5.8 – Passing the set income test

The results show that the `SetIncome, given initial render, displays budget summary values` test passes as expected in the previous code. Now you know how to refactor tests created with the `ReactTestUtils` module. The skills learned in this section will arm you with the knowledge to refactor legacy test code to use modern testing tools.

Refactoring tests to comply with common testing best practices

In the previous section, we learned how to refactor tests created with ReactTestUtils. In this section, we will cover a few scenarios where we can refactor existing test code to be more robust and maintainable. We will use the following feedback form application to illustrate examples:

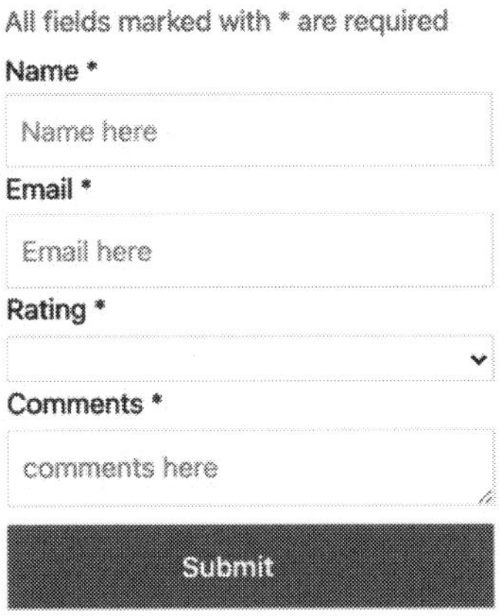

Figure 5.9 – Feedback form

In the preceding screenshot, we have a form for users to complete the **Name** and **Email** fields, as well as select a rating, enter comments, and finally, submit their information. If a user tries to submit the form with blank values for the required fields, an error message is displayed:

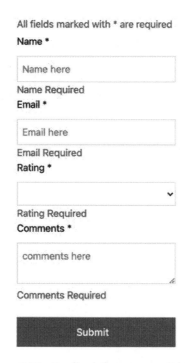

Figure 5.10 – Feedback form error validation

In the preceding screenshot, form validation errors are displayed under each input with blank values. Finally, when a user submits the form with valid input data, a **Thank you** message is displayed:

We appreciate your responses John Doe!

Figure 5.11 – Submitted feedback form

In the preceding screenshot, the message **We appreciate your responses John Doe!** is displayed. The **John Doe** part of the message is the value entered for the **Name** input element in the form. The first test we will refactor verifies that an error message is displayed when invalid emails are entered:

```
test.each`
  value
  ${'a'}
```

```
${'a@b'}
${'a@b.c'}
`('displays error message', async ({ value }) => {
```

In the preceding code, first, the each method from Jest was used to run the same test with different values: a, a@b, and a@b.c. Next, we see the test name, displays error message. The test name is vague because it does not provide enough details regarding the context of the test. It is common to use test naming conventions to eliminate issues with vague test names. There are many popular naming conventions, such as when_ stateUnderTest_expect_expectedBehavior and given_preconditions_ when_stateUnderTest_then_expectedBehavior, that describe the code under test, the actions performed on the code, and finally, the expected result. The important thing to remember is to use a naming convention in agreement with your project team.

We will use the following convention, component under test, given preconditions, expected results, in our refactoring efforts. We can refactor the current test name like so:

```
'Form, given invalid email value "$value", displays error
    message',
```

In the preceding code, we refactor the current test name to Form, given invalid email value "$value", displays error message. When reading the test name, it is clear now that we are testing a Form component, the given preconditions are invalid values, and the expected result is to see an error message on the screen. Notice the $value variable in the test name. The variable will be replaced with the name of the current value for each test iteration, further providing context to understand the specific test code.

Next, we will analyze and refactor the main test code:

```
async ({ value }) => {
    const { getByRole, getByText } = render(<App />)
    const emailInput = getByRole('textbox', { name: /email/i })

    user.click(emailInput)
    user.tab()
    user.type(emailInput, value)

    await waitFor(() => {
        const errorMessage = getByText(/invalid email address/i)
```

```
        expect(errorMessage).toBeInTheDocument()
    })
  }
)
```

In the preceding code, the object destructuring approach was used to access the `getByRole` and `getByText` query methods. However, the destructing approach requires you to manually keep track of which queries to add or remove as you build out the test code. As mentioned in *Chapter 1, Exploring React Testing Library*, we can use the `screen` object to access query methods starting in version **9** of React Testing Library.

Using the `screen` object to access query methods is easier to maintain and results in cleaner code than the destructuring approach. The `waitFor` method is also used to grab and verify that the error message is displayed asynchronously in the DOM. However, the `findBy*` queries of the `screen` object are also asynchronous and are easier-to-use options than `waitFor` when you need to query elements that take time to appear on the screen. We can refactor the current test code like so:

```
async ({ value }) => {
  render(<App />)
  const emailInput = screen.getByRole('textbox', { name: /
    email/i })

  user.click(emailInput)
  user.tab()
  user.type(emailInput, value)

  const errorMessage = await screen.findByText(/invalid email
    address/i)
  expect(errorMessage).toBeInTheDocument()
}
)
```

In the preceding code, we replaced the destructured queries to access via the screen object. We also replaced the `waitFor` method with an asynchronous `findByText` query. Now the test code is cleaner and easier to maintain.

The next test we will refactor verifies that an error message is displayed when a user doesn't enter a value for any required form input:

```
test('Form, given blank input value, displays error message',
   async () => {
   render(<App />)
   const nameInput = screen.getByRole('textbox', { name: /name/i
})
   const emailInput = screen.getByRole('textbox', { name: /
      email/i })
   const ratingSelect = screen.getByRole('combobox', { name: /
      rating/i })
   const commentsInput = screen.getByRole('textbox', { name: /
      comments/i })
```

In the preceding code, first, the application is rendered in the DOM. Next, the test is arranged by grabbing all the form input elements and storing them in respective values. Next, actions are performed on the form elements:

```
user.click(nameInput)
user.click(emailInput)
user.click(ratingSelect)
user.click(commentsInput)
user.tab()
```

In the preceding code, each input element is clicked. Then, pressing the *Tab* key on the keyboard simulates to move the focus away from the actively selected ratingSelect element. Finally, four assertions are made:

```
expect(await screen.findByText(/name required/i)).
   toBeInTheDocument()
expect(await screen.findByText(/email required/i)).
   toBeInTheDocument()
expect(await screen.findByText(/rating required/i)).
   toBeInTheDocument()
expect(await screen.findByText(/comments required/i)).
   toBeInTheDocument()
```

In the preceding code, an assertion is made to verify that specific error messages are displayed for empty form values. However, if, for example, the first assertion for the **name required** error message fails, the test fails and none of the other assertions will be made. This approach of multiple assertions in the same test is not a good practice because we will not know whether the code for the remaining assertions works as expected.

Each assertion in the test is independent of other assertions, and therefore, should live inside their own individual test. We can refactor the test like so:

```
test.each`
  inputLabel
  ${'Name'}
  ${'Email'}
  ${'Rating'}
  ${'Comments'}
`(
  'Form, given blank $inputLabel input value, displays error message',
```

In the preceding code, first, we use the `each` method to create individual tests for the **Name**, **Email**, **Rating**, and **Comments** `input` element names. The input names will be passed to the `inputLabel` variable for each test run. Next, we will write the main test code:

```
async ({ inputLabel }) => {
  render(<App />)

  user.click(screen.getByText(`${inputLabel} *`))
  user.tab()

  const errorMessage = await screen.findByText(`${inputLabel}
    Required`)
  expect(errorMessage).toBeInTheDocument()
}
)
```

In the preceding code, first, we render the App component in the DOM. Next, we click the input label using getByText. Then, we simulate pressing the *Tab* key to move the focus away from the input element. Finally, we grab the element with the error message, store it in the errorMessage variable, and verify that it is in the DOM. We get the following output when we run the refactored tests:

Figure 5.12 – Feedback form test results

In the preceding screenshot, all refactored test cases pass as expected. Now you know how to refactor tests to use testing best practices of naming conventions and splitting multiple assertions from one test into individual tests. You also learned how to refactor legacy tests written in React Testing Library to modern approaches.

Summary

In this chapter, you have learned how to reduce the burden of updating production dependencies of legacy applications. You learned how to refactor legacy tests using the modern React Testing Library tool. You also learned a few testing best practices. The skills acquired in this chapter should give you the confidence that you can successfully refactor outdated code to current versions without significant issues. You should also be able to refactor test code to be more maintainable.

In the next chapter, we will learn about additional tools and plugins for testing.

Questions

1. Explain the benefits of using React Testing Library compared to tools such as Enzyme or ReactTestUtils.

2. Explain the benefits of running tests in Jest's watch mode.

3. When should you use the each method from Jest when writing tests?

6

Implementing Additional Tools and Plugins for Testing

In the previous chapters, we learned the basics of React Testing Library and how to test from simple to complex components using the tool. In this chapter, we will learn how to increase our productivity by using additional tools. We will install and use a few plugins to help our ability to write tests by avoiding common mistakes and following React Testing Library's best practices.

We will add a library to audit and increase application accessibility. We'll ensure we select the best React Testing Library query method with Testing Playground. Finally, we will increase our productivity by using Wallaby.js to receive rapid feedback on our tests' status from our code editor.

In this chapter, we're going to cover the following main topics:

- Using `eslint-plugin-testing-library` to follow best practices and avoid common mistakes when using React Testing Library

- Using `eslint-plugin-jest-dom` to follow best practices and avoid common mistakes when using `jest-dom`

- Using `jest-axe` to increase application accessibility
- Selecting the Testing Library-recommended queries with Testing Playground
- Increasing our testing productivity with Wallaby.js

The skills in this chapter will increase your productivity and enhance your ability to test React applications using Testing Library's best practices.

Technical requirements

For the examples in this chapter, you will need to have Node.js installed on your machine. We will be using the `create-react-app` CLI tool for all code examples. Please familiarize yourself with the tool before starting this chapter, if required. Code snippets will be provided throughout the chapter to understand the code under test, but the objective is to understand how to test the code.

You can find code examples for this chapter at `https://github.com/PacktPublishing/Simplify-Testing-with-React-Testing-Library/tree/master/Chapter06`.

Implementing best practices with Testing Library ESLint plugins

In this section, you will learn how to install and use `eslint-plugin-testing-library` and `eslint-plugin-jest-dom`. The purpose of these plugins is to audit your test code and help you to write tests that follow the best practices of **Document Object Model** (**DOM**) Testing Library and `jest-dom`. The plugins work by highlighting areas that can be improved and providing recommendations to refactor your code.

Before installing the plugins, we need to have **ESLint** installed in our project. ESLint is a tool that statistically analyzes and informs you of problems in your code. You can think of ESLint as having someone look over your shoulder to point out issues you might otherwise take longer to debug on your own. For example, you could create the following function:

```
const reverseWord = str => str.split('').reverse().join('')
```

In the preceding code, we have a `reverseWord` function that reverses a passed-in string. If we invoke the function with the word `packt`, we get the following result:

```
reverseWord('packt') // tkcap
```

In the preceding code, we get a result of tkcap when we pass in packt as a parameter to the function. However, if we mistakenly misspell the function name and run the code, we get the following result:

Figure 6.1 – The reverseWord function name typo

In the previous code, the console output indicates ReferenceError. The error refers to the interpreter not locating a defined function, called reverseeWord, in the file. The problem was that the user mistakenly added an extra e in the function name. We could create a better workflow by installing and configuring ESLint in our project to help debug issues.

If you are using create-react-app for your project, then ESLint should automatically be installed for you. For projects that don't already have ESLint installed, use the following command:

```
npm install eslint --save-dev
```

The previous command will install ESLint as a development dependency to your project.

Next, we can create a configuration file to tell ESLint how we want it to lint our files:

```
{
    "extends": "eslint:recommended",
    "parserOptions": {
        "ecmaVersion": 2021,
        "sourceType": "module"
    }
}
```

The configuration file that was created in json format, in the previous code, has a few settings that tell ESLint how to lint our files. The "extends" key is set to "eslint:recommended". This means that we want to use ESLint's recommended linting rules. The "parserOptions" key is set to an object with two keys. The "ecmaVersion" key is set to **2021**. This means that the code we write will support JavaScript options available in the 2021 version of ECMAScript. The "sourceType" key is set to "module", meaning our code will support ES modules. There are numerous ways ESLint can be configured to lint your project files.

> **Note**
>
> Please refer to *Configuring ESLint* (`https://eslint.org/docs/user-guide/configuring/`) for more details.

Use the following command to run ESLint against your project files:

```
npx eslint .
```

In the previous command, we use the `npx` command to run ESLint against all of the project files. Note that `npx` allows you to quickly execute `npm` packages regardless of whether the package is installed locally or globally on your machine or not installed at all. We receive the following output in the console after running the command:

```
  1:7  error  'reverseWord' is assigned a value but never used  no-unused-vars
  3:1  error  'reverseeWord' is not defined                     no-undef

× 2 problems (2 errors, 0 warnings)
```

Figure 6.2 – ESLint output

In the previous command, ESLint informs us of two errors in our code. The first error says that the `reverseWord` function was never used on line `1`, referencing the `no-unused-vars` ESLint rule. The second error says that `reverseeWord` on line `3` is not defined anywhere in the file, referencing the `no-undef` ESLint rule. We can also enhance our ESLint workflow by displaying the output directly in our code editor to learn about any potential issues before running our code. For example, the VSCode and Atom code editors have third-party tools that we can install to display problems directly in the editor.

> **Note**
>
> Please refer to *ESLint* (`https://marketplace.visualstudio.com/items?itemName=dbaeumer.vscode-eslint`) for the VSCode editor extension. Alternatively, you can refer to *linter-eslint* (`https://atom.io/packages/linter-eslint`) for the Atom editor plugin for installation and configuration details.

Displaying the linter output directly in the code editor provides faster feedback than manually running ESLint via the command line. Now that you understand how to get ESLint up and running, we will install and configure `eslint-plugin-testing-library` in the next section.

Installing and configuring eslint-plugin-testing-library

In this section, we will learn how to install and configure `eslint-plugin-testing-library` inside our application. Install the plugin using the following command:

```
npm install --save-dev eslint-plugin-testing-library
```

The preceding command installs `eslint-plugin-testing-library` as a development dependency in your project. Now that the plugin is installed, we can add it to our ESLint configuration file:

```
"overrides": [
  {
    "files": ["*.test.js"],
    "extends": [
      "plugin:testing-library/react"
    ]
```

In the previous code, we created an `"overrides"` section in our ESLint configuration to target any files ending in `.test.js`. Then, we added `plugin:testing-library/react` to the `extends` array in the configuration file. We added the React version of the plugin to gain React-specific rules and the rules we get from DOM Testing Library's base rules. The plugin applies a particular set of linting rules that are specific to React applications. For example, the `no-dom-import` rule, which doesn't allow direct imports from DOM Testing Library, is useful because React Testing Library re-exports everything from DOM Testing Library, eliminating the need for direct imports.

> **Note**
>
> Please refer to *Supported Rules* (`https://github.com/testing-library/eslint-plugin-testing-library#supported-rules`) for a complete list of React-specific applied rules.

Note that the `react-app` entry is also included in the array. The `react-app` entry adds ESLint rules that have been set up by `create-react-app`. Now that we have the plugin set up in the project, we can write tests. We will test a drop-down component that allows a user to select a programming language:

Figure 6.3 – The drop-down component

In the preceding screenshot, you can see a dropdown that lists four programing languages that a user can click on to choose. When a user selects a language, we get the following:

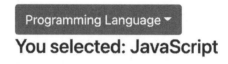

Figure 6.4 – The selected drop-down option

Here, you can view the text **You selected: JavaScript**, which appears when a user selects the **JavaScript** option. We can write a test to verify that the selected language displays on the screen:

```
test('LanguageDropdown, given selected menu item, displays
    selection', async () => {
  render(<LanguageDropdown />)


  user.click(screen.getByRole('button', { name: /programming
language/I }))
```

```
  user.click(screen.getByRole''menuite'', { name: /javascript/i
}))
```

```
  user.click(screen.getByRole''menuite'', { name: /javascript/i
}))
```

In the preceding code, first, we render the `LanguageDropdown` component in the DOM. Next, we click on the **Programming Language** button. Then, we select **JavaScript** from the menu options. Next, we will verify that the selected option is displayed on the screen:

```
const selection = await waitFor(() =>
    screen.getByRole('heading', { name: /you selected:
      javascript/i })
)
```

In the preceding code, we use the `waitFor` method from React Testing Library to get the element with the text that includes the selected option. The `waitFor` method can be used when you need to wait for an element in the DOM. However, according to `eslint-plugin-testing-library`, `waitFor` is not the best way to select an element in this situation:

```
(alias) const screen: Screen<typeof queries>
import screen

Prefer findByRole method over using await waitFor(() =>
    screen.getByRole('heading', { name: /you selected:
javascript/i })
  ) eslint(testing-library/prefer-find-by)
Peek Problem (⌥F8)   Quick Fix... (⌘.)
    screen.getByRole('heading', { name: /you selected: javascript/i })
  )
```

Figure 6.5 – The findByRole linter suggestion

In the previous screenshot, the code that includes the `waitFor` method is underlined by ESLint, drawing our attention to the code issue. When we hover over the `waitFor` method code, we get feedback indicating that the preferred query is `findByRole` via the `prefer-find-by` rule of `eslint-plugin-testing-library`.

In *Chapter 5, Refactoring Legacy Applications with React Testing Library*, we learned how to use the `findByRole` query to select elements that need time to appear on the screen. The `prefer-find-by` rule is a `fixable` rule; this means that we can select to have the problem code automatically fixed for us.

One easy way to automatically fix issues is by setting up your code editor to automatically resolve any fixable issues when saving a file. Please refer to the documentation of your respective code editor for instructions. If, for some reason, your editor does not have a *fix on save* feature, you can run `eslint --fix` in the command line or use pre-commit hooks via `git`. As a last resort, you always have the option of referring to the `eslint-plugin-testing-library` documentation, which is related to the `prefer-find-by` rule and others, for suggestions. Once we refactor the problem code, we get the following output:

```
const selection = await screen.findByRole('heading', {
  name: /you selected: javascript/i
})

expect(selection).toBeInTheDocument()
})
```

In the preceding code, the `waitFor` code is replaced with the `findByRole` query method. The code has a cleaner syntax that behaves similarly to the `waitFor` code and satisfies the linter rules. Finally, we assert that the selected code is in the document.

Some rules are not automatically enabled with the React version of `eslint-plugin-testing-library`. For example, in previous versions of React Testing Library, it was common to see selectors written as follows:

```
const { getByRole } = render(<LanguageDropdown />)

user.click(getByRole('button', { name: /programming
  language/i }))
user.click(getByRole('menuitem', { name: /javascript/i }))
```

In the preceding code, we access the query methods by destructuring them off the rendered component. The latest React Testing Library versions suggest using the `screen` object to access query methods for a better user experience. The `screen` object allows you to access query methods using your editor's autocomplete feature rather than undergoing explicit destructuring via the rendered component. We can add the `prefer-screen-queries` rule to our ESLint configuration file to enforce this way of selecting query methods:

```
"rules": {
  "testing-library/prefer-screen-queries": "error"
}
```

In the preceding code, we added a `"rules"` key to the configuration file. The `"rules"` key is used when we want to add specific rules to enforce our code. Inside the `"rules"` key, we add the `"testing-library/prefer-screen-queries"` key, which is set to `"error"`. If we had our project set up with a linting script to run ESLint across our files, the error would trigger an exit code to stop file execution, making it clear that the current code is not acceptable for use.

Now, with this rule in place, the previous code using destructuring will be flagged by ESLint:

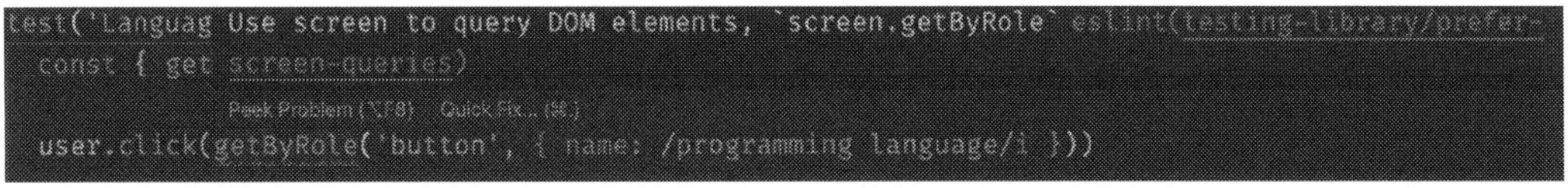

```
test('Languag Use screen to query DOM elements, `screen.getByRole` eslint(testing-library/prefer-
  const { get screen-queries)
            Peek Problem (⌥F8)   Quick Fix... (⌘.)
  user.click(getByRole('button', { name: /programming language/i }))
```

Figure 6.6 – The prefer-screen-queries linter suggestion

In the previous screenshot, `getByRole` is underlined by ESLint to draw our attention to the query issue. When we hover over the query, we get feedback indicating that the preferred approach uses `screen` to query DOM elements via the `prefer-screen-queries` rule of `eslint-plugin-testing-library`.

Unlike the `prefer-find-by` rule in the previous example, `prefer-screen-queries` is not a *fixable* rule. This means that we will need to fix the code manually. When we refactor the code, we get the following result:

```
render(<LanguageDropdown />)
user.click(screen.getByRole('button', { name: /programming
  language/i }))
user.click(screen.getByRole('menuitem', { name: /javascript/i
}))
```

The DOM selectors have been refactored to use the `screen` object in the preceding code, satisfying the `prefer-screen-queries` rule. The code also looks cleaner compared to the version using destructured query methods.

In some situations, we might want rules that provide a warning compared to an error when ESLint runs across project files. The warning won't stop code execution; however, instead, it will serve as a reminder to the user to remove the file's highlighted code before committing the code. For example, it is common to use the `debug` method to view the current state of the DOM as we build tests:

```
render(<LanguageDropdown />)
screen.debug()
```

In the previous code, the debug method is used for logging the current DOM output to the console after rendering the LanguageDropdown component. The debug method will be highlighted in the editor, as follows:

```
test('Lan Unexpected debug statement eslint(testing-library/no-debug)
  render( Peek Problem (⌥F8)   Quick Fix... (⌘.)
  screen.debug()
```

Figure 6.7 – The no-debug linter suggestion

In the preceding screenshot, debug is underlined by ESLint to draw our attention to an issue with the query. When we hover over the query, we get feedback indicating the method should be removed via the no-debug rule of eslint-plugin-testing-library. We often forget to remove the console's logging code before committing work, so the no-debug rule serves as a helpful reminder to remove it.

Now you know how to install and configure ESLint with eslint-plugin-testing-library to help avoid issues and follow best practices while writing tests.

In the next section, we will go a step further by installing another plugin that is specific to jest-dom.

Installing and configuring eslint-plugin-jest-dom

In the previous section, we installed and configured ESLint and eslint-plugin-testing-library. In this section, we will teach you how to install and configure eslint-plugin-jest-dom, ensuring we follow the best practices using jest-dom. Use the following command to install the plugin:

```
npm install --save-dev eslint-plugin-jest-dom
```

The previous command installs eslint-plugin-jest-dom as a development dependency inside the project. Now that the plugin is installed, we can add it to our ESLint configuration file:

```
{
  "extends": ["react-app", "plugin:jest-dom/recommended"]
}
```

In the previous code, we added `plugin:jest-dom/recommended` to the `extends` array in the configuration file. The `recommended` configuration for the plugin is used to automatically include a set of standard rules to enforce `jest-dom` best practices. We will test a `checkbox` component that allows the user to select their preferred programming languages:

Select Preferred Languages
☐ JavaScript ☐ Ruby ☐ Java ☐ C#

Figure 6.8 – The languages checkbox component

In the preceding screenshot, you can see that there are four checkboxes for programming languages that a user can select from. When a user selects a language, we get the following:

Select Preferred Languages
☑ JavaScript ☐ Ruby ☐ Java ☐ C#

Figure 6.9 – The selected language checkbox

In the preceding screenshot, the user selects **JavaScript**, which results in the associated checkbox being selected, the text color changing to *green,* and the font-weight changing to *bold.* We can write a test to verify that the checkbox for the selected language is selected and has the expected classes associated with the color and font-weight of the text the user sees on the screen:

```
test('LanguageCheckbox, given selected item, item is checked',
  () => {
  render(<LanguageCheckBox />)
  const jsCheckbox = screen.getByRole('checkbox', { name: /
    javascript/i })

  user.click(jsCheckbox)
```

In the preceding code, we render the `LanguageCheckBox` component to the DOM. Next, we get the **JavaScript** checkbox, store it in the `jsCheckbox` variable, and click on it. Next, we will make assertions on the expected output. First, we try using the `toHaveAttribute` Jest matcher:

```
expect(jsCheckbox).toHaveAttribute("checked");
```

In the preceding code, we use `toHaveAttribute` to verify that the checkbox has the `checked` attribute after being clicked. However, our test will fail with this matcher because it only looks for an explicit `checked` attribute that is added to the elements commonly used in situations where we want a prechecked checkbox. In our case, we're testing the result of a user clicking on the checkbox in the resulting DOM, so we need a different matcher. Next, we try using the `toHaveProperty` Jest matcher:

```
expect(jsCheckbox).toHaveProperty("checked", true);
```

In the preceding code, we use the `toHaveProperty` Jest matcher to verify that the checkbox has the `checked` property set to `true`. This matcher works in a technical sense, but it doesn't read very clearly. Additionally, when we hover over the matcher, we get the following output:

```
                              Use toBeChecked() instead of
                              toHaveProperty("checked", true) eslint(jest-
user.click(jsChecl            dom/prefer-checked)

expect(jsCheckbox).toHaveProperty("checked", true);
```

Figure 6.10 – The prefer-checked linter suggestion

In the preceding screenshot, the `toHaveProperty` matcher is underlined by ESLint to draw our attention to the matcher's issue. When we hover over the matcher, we get feedback indicating it should be replaced with the `jest-dom` `toBeChecked` matcher via the `prefer-checked` rule of `eslint-plugin-jest-dom`. The rule is automatically fixable and will refactor the matcher for us if we have our code editor set up. When we refactor our matcher, we get the following output:

```
expect(jsCheckbox).toBeChecked()
```

In the preceding code, we use the `toBeChecked` `jest-dom` matcher to verify that the checkbox is checked. Now we have a matcher that eliminates any issues with previous matcher versions and also reads a lot better. Next, we will assert the expected classes:

```
expect(screen.getByText(/javascript/i).className).
    toContain('text-success font-weight-bold')
```

In the preceding code, we access the `className` property inside the element with the `javascript` text to verify that it contains the `text-success` and `font-weight-bold` classes. However, when we hover over `toContain`, we get the following feedback:

```
                              Prefer .toHaveClass() over checking element
                       className eslint(jest-dom/prefer-to-have-class)
expect(jsCheckbox).toBeC
expect(screen.getByText(/javascript/i).className).toContain('text-succes
```

Figure 6.11 – The prefer-to-have-class linter suggestion

In the preceding screenshot, the `toContain` matcher is underlined by ESLint to draw our attention to the matcher's issue. When we hover over the matcher, we get feedback indicating that it should be replaced with the `jest-dom toHaveClass` matcher via the `prefer-to-have-class` rule of `eslint-plugin-jest-dom`. Similar to the previous example, the `prefer-to-have-class` rule is automatically fixable and will refactor the matcher for us if we have our code editor set up to do so. When we refactor the code, we get the following output:

```
expect(screen.getByText(/javascript/i)).toHaveClass(
    'text-success font-weight-bold'
)
```

In the preceding code, we refactored our code to use the `jest-dom toHaveClass` matcher. Now we have a matcher that is easier to implement and read compared to our original example.

Now you understand how to install and use the `eslint-plugin-jest-dom` plugin to use assertion matchers that follow the `jest-dom` best practices. In the next section, we will learn how to install and use a package to increase the accessibility of our component's source code.

Testing accessibility with jest-axe

In this section, we will learn how to use a tool that is designed to help improve the accessibility of our features. There are many tools available that can help increase accessibility by automating the process of auditing and reporting issues, such as Wave (`https://wave.webaim.org/`) and Lighthouse (`https://developers.google.com/web/tools/lighthouse`). However, there is no single tool that can guarantee accessibility across an entire application. Accessibility auditing tools are helpful, but they do not replace the need for manual accessibility auditing done by a human. For example, when an abbreviation is used for the first time in a line of text, the related expanded version should be included:

```
Structured Query Language (SQL) is used to manage data in
relational databases.
```

In the preceding sentence, the expanded version, `Structured Query Language`, is included with its abbreviated form, `SQL`. The sentence would need to be manually checked to verify accessibility. We will learn how to use `jest-axe`, which is a tool that adds a custom matcher for Jest and behaves in ways that are similar to ESLint. The tool helps find and report common accessibility issues in your code, such as image buttons with no alternate text or `inputs` with no associated labels. Use the following command to install the tool:

```
npm install --save-dev jest-axe
```

The previous command installs `jest-axe` as a development dependency inside the project. Now that the tool is installed, we can use it in our tests. First, we will test the accessibility of an image button:

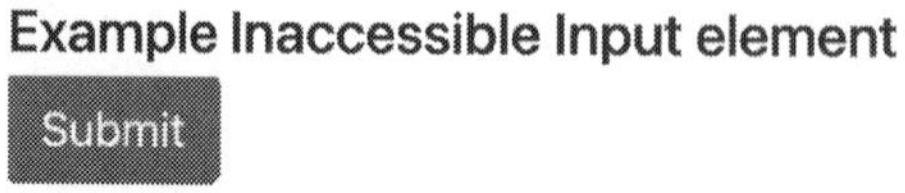

Example Inaccessible Input element

Submit

Figure 6.12 – An inaccessible image button

In the preceding screenshot, we have an image that behaves as a **Submit** button. The following is the source code for the image button:

```
import loginImg from './image/login.png'
<input src={loginImg} type="image" />
```

In the preceding code, we will import an image and pass it as `source` for an input of the `image` type. Now we will write a test to verify that the element is accessible to users:

```
import { render } from '@testing-library/react'
import { axe } from 'jest-axe'
import 'jest-axe/extend-expect'
import NoAccessibility from './NoAccessibility'
```

In the preceding code, first, we import the `render` method from React Testing Library. Then, we import the `axe` method from `jest-axe`. The `axe` method is what we will use to audit the accessibility of our component. Next, we import `jest-axe/extend-expect`, which adds a special matcher to Jest to report the audit outcome in a readable format. Finally, we import the `NoAccessibility` component to test. Next, we will write the main test code:

```
const { container } = render(<NoAccessibility />)
const results = await axe(container)
expect(results).toHaveNoViolations()
```

In the preceding code, first, we destructure `container` off the rendered component. Unlike query methods, we can destructure `container` off the rendered component without violating DOM Testing Library's best practices because it is not available on the `screen` object. `container` is the `div` element that wraps your React component under test.

Next, we pass `container` as an argument to the `axe` method and store it in the `results` variable. The `axe` method will run an accessibility audit across our component under test. Finally, we assert that the results have no accessibility issues using the `toHaveNoViolations` matcher. The test will pass if no violations are found.

However, if violations are found, the test will fail and provide feedback to resolve those issues. When we run the test, we get the following output:

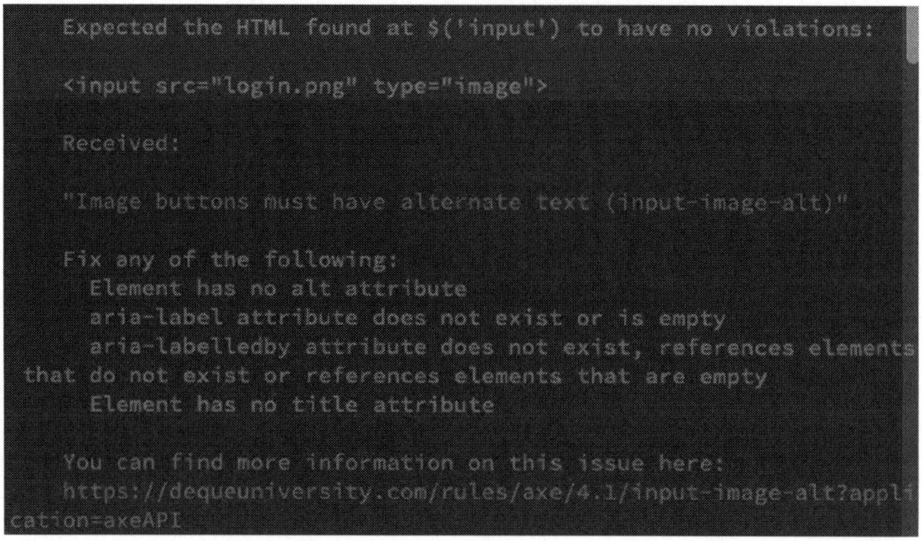

Figure 6.13 – Inaccessible image button test output

The preceding screenshot shows that accessibility violations were found in the `NoAccessibility` component, which resulted in a test failure with feedback. First, the feedback indicates that an `input` element is the source of the issue. Next, we see the entire element printed on the screen. Then, we get the `"Image buttons must have alternate text (input-image-alt)"` message, informing us why the element failed the audit. Next, we get several suggestions that we can implement to resolve the issue. Finally, we get a hyperlink that we can follow to gain a deeper understanding of the issue. We will resolve the issue by providing an `alt` attribute:

```
<input src={loginImg} type="image" alt="login" />
```

In the preceding code, we added an `alt` attribute with the value of `login`. Now, when we rerun our test, we get the following result:

Figure 6.14 – Accessible image button test output

In the preceding screenshot, the test results indicate that NoAccessibility, given accessibility audit, returns no violations passes with no violations. Next, we will test the accessibility of a list that includes an image:

Example Inaccessible Unordered List

- Building with React
- Testing with React Testing Library

Figure 6.15 – An inaccessible list

In the preceding screenshot, we have an unordered list that includes an image element. The following is the source code for the list:

```
<ul>
    <li>Building with React</li>
    <li>Testing with React Testing Library</li>
    <img
      src="http://unsplash.it/g/200?random&gravity=center"
      alt="tulips"
    />
</ul>
```

In the preceding code, we have an unordered list element with two list item child elements and one image child element. Our test code will be the same as the previous test for the image button. The only difference here is the component that we pass into the render method. So, for this example, we will only focus on the test results:

```
Expected the HTML found at $('ul') to have no violations:

<ul><li>Building with React</li><li>Testing with React Testing Library</li><img src=
tp://unsplash.it/g/200?random&amp;gravity=center" alt="tulips"></ul>

Received:

"<ul> and <ol> must only directly contain <li>, <script> or <template> elements (list)"

Fix all of the following:
  List element has direct children that are not allowed inside <li> elements

You can find more information on this issue here:
https://dequeuniversity.com/rules/axe/4.1/list?application=axeAPI
```

Figure 6.16 – Inaccessible list test results

The preceding screenshot shows that accessibility violations were found in the unordered list component, which resulted in a test failure with feedback. First, the feedback indicates that a ul element is the source of the issue. Next, we see the entire element printed on the screen. Then, we get the "<ul> and <ol> must only directly contain <li>, <script> or <template> elements (list)" message, which helps us to understand why the element failed the audit.

Next, we get a suggestion regarding how to resolve the issue. Finally, we get a hyperlink that we can follow to gain a deeper understanding of the issue. We will resolve the issue by moving the image inside an li element:

```
<ul>
    <li>Building with React</li>
    <li>Testing with React Testing Library</li>
    <li>
      <img
        src="http://unsplash.it/ g/200?random&
            gravity=center"
        alt="tulips"
      />
    </li>
</ul>
```

In the previous code, we wrapped the `image` element inside an `li` element. When we rerun our test, the test will pass and return results that are similar to what we saw in the image button's previous test. Now you know how to use `jest-axe` to increase the accessibility of applications using React with Jest. It is important to reiterate that automated accessibility tools help increase our applications' ability to work for various end users. However, they cannot catch all issues and are not a replacement for manual audits.

Next, we will learn how to use a tool to speed up our element selections with React Testing Library.

Selecting the best queries with Testing Playground

In this section, we will learn how to use **Testing Playground**. This is a tool that makes it easier for you to determine the right DOM Testing Library query selector. Testing Playground allows you to paste HTML into an interactive website, which allows you to click on elements as they appear rendered in the browser. This enables you to learn which DOM Testing Library queries can be used to select a particular element.

The tool always suggests queries in order, based on the DOM Testing Library query recommendations for elements that offer multiple ways of selection. Furthermore, the tool allows you to copy the selector to use in your test code. We will look at two ways of using Testing Playground: first, via the website, and second, via a Chrome extension.

Selecting queries using the Testing Playground website

In this section, we will learn how to use Testing Playground via its website. In previous examples throughout the book, we used the `debug` method to log the resulting HTML of components to the console while writing tests. One limitation of the `debug` method is that it has no feature that enables you to log the output to the browser and test out different query methods to select elements.

We can use the `logTestingPlaygroundURL` method inside a test file to log the resulting HTML to a browser via *Testing Playground* (`https://testing-playground.com/`) and utilize the site's query selector features. For example, we could be in the process of selecting elements in a test for the following `MoreInfoPopover` component:

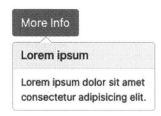

Figure 6.17 – The Popover component

In the preceding screenshot, we have a `button` element with the text **More Info**, which displays a popover with dummy text when it is clicked on. We want to select the `button` element using DOM Testing Library queries, so we start our test as follows:

```
import { render, screen } from '@testing-library/react'
import MoreInfoPopover from './MoreInfoPopover'

it('logs output to Testing Playground', () => {
  render(<MoreInfoPopover />)
  screen.logTestingPlaygroundURL()
})
```

We import the `render` and `screen` methods from React Testing Library and the component under test in the preceding code. Inside the main test code, first, we render the component in the DOM. Next, we call the `logTestingPlaygroundURL` method. When we run the test, we get the following output:

```
console.log
    Open this URL in your browser

    https://testing-playground.com/#markup=DwEwlgbgfKkAQGcAuBPANgUw
LwCIC2AhgE4DmYAdgFxwCsADgB4DcOMARgK5JID25cqOthydufHHDAhceHkQwBJcgDM
eEgMZoCCBLjZJ++8gFo6RMISIpWAWTkY4S1cAD0o3uRgvw0Vz6hAA

        at Object.logTestingPlaygroundURL (node_modules/@testing-libr
ary/dom/dist/screen.js:47:11)
```

Figure 6.18 – The Testing Playground link

In the preceding screenshot, we have a unique link to the Testing Playground website to follow and view our component's rendered HTML. When we follow the link, we should see something similar to the following:

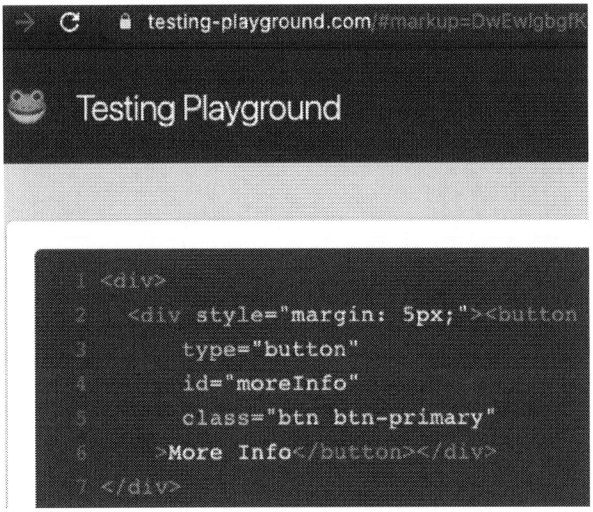

```
→  C   🔒 testing-playground.com/#markup=DwEwlgbgfK

🐸  Testing Playground


1 <div>
2    <div style="margin: 5px;"><button
3       type="button"
4       id="moreInfo"
5       class="btn btn-primary"
6     >More Info</button></div>
7 </div>
```

Figure 6.19 – The Testing Playground HTML structure

In the preceding screenshot, the link navigated us to the Testing Playground website. First, we see a section that includes the HTML structure for our component. Next, we see the rendered browser output, as follows:

Figure 6.20 – The Testing Playground browser output

In the preceding screenshot, we can see a section with the browser output for our component. Notice that we don't see the complete result with associated styles included. The Testing Playground website only displays the HTML content. Next, we see a **suggested query** section, as follows:

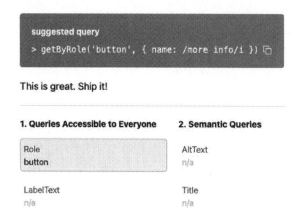

Figure 6.21 – Testing Playground suggested query

In the preceding screenshot, we get a **suggested query** for the button element we clicked on in the browser output section. The getByRole query is the best way to select the button based on its HTML structure. Additionally, we can see the **This is great. Ship it!** message, which suggests that we should use this query further.

There are also other options available, as shown in the following screenshot, to select the element:

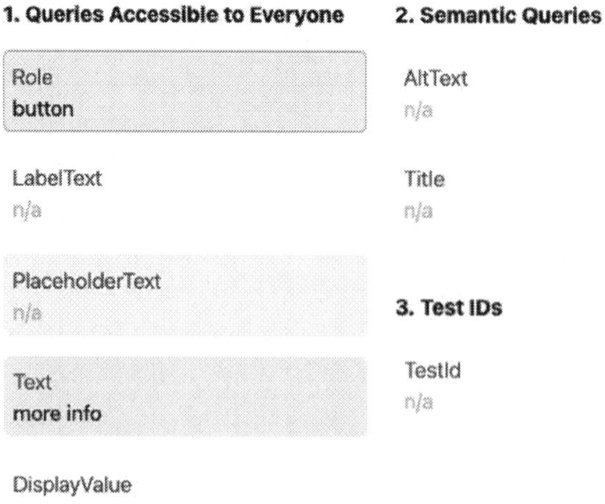

Figure 6.22 – Testing Playground query priority options

In the preceding code, we can see multiple options to select the element in order of priority. Based on the HTML structure of the `button` element, there are two ways we could choose the element – *by its role* and *by its text value*. The other listed queries are not available for the button and, therefore, display **n/a**. If we decide to select the **Text** query option, we should see something similar to the following screenshot:

```
suggested query
> getByRole('button', { name: /more info/i })
```

Figure 6.23 – The Testing Playground text query option

In the preceding screenshot, we can see the text **Nice! getByText is a great selector! Using getByRole would still be preferable though.**. This message informs us that while it is not wrong to use `getByText` to select the button, it is not the best query for the selected element. Once we decide on the query we want to grab the element, we can click on the icon displayed on the far right of the **suggested query** box to copy the code needed to select the element within our test.

Now you know how to use the `logTestingPlaygroundURL` method to select elements using the Testing Playground website. There is one notable limitation to using the Testing Playground website. When we click on the **More Info** button, we should see a popup appear beneath the button. We cannot use the Testing Playground website to perform this action since it only copies the HTML and not the associated JavaScript to render the result of clicking on the button.

In the next section, we will learn how to use the Testing Playground Chrome extension to overcome this limitation.

Selecting queries using the Testing Playground Chrome extension

In this section, we will install and use the Testing Playground Chrome extension to overcome the limitations of using the Testing Playground website. This extension provides the benefit of allowing you to use Testing Playground features locally, in the same browser that is used to run your application. The extension is currently only available for the Google Chrome browser, so be sure to install it if necessary.

Install the *Testing Playground Chrome extension* (`https://chrome.`
`google.com/webstore/detail/testing-playground/`
`hejbmebodbijjdhflfknehhcgaklhano`) via the Chrome Web Store. Once
the extension is installed, a new **Testing Playground** tab is added to your **Chrome
Developer Tools**.

Going back to the `MoreInfoPopover` component from the previous section, we can write
a test to verify that the popover is displayed when a user clicks on the **More Info** button:

```
test('MoreInfoPopover, given clicked button, displays popover',
  () => {
  render(<MoreInfoPopover />)
```

In the preceding code, we render `MoreInfoPopover` in the DOM. Next, we will use the
Testing Playground extension to find the preferred query selector for the button:

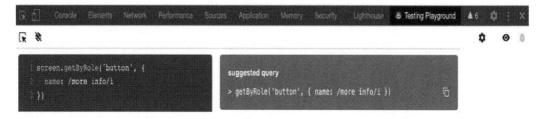

Figure 6.24 – The Testing Playground Chrome extension

In the previous screenshot, we can see a tab added for the **Testing Playground** extension
in the **Chrome Developer Tools**. The experience of using the Chrome extension is
similar to that of the Testing Playground website. However, now, we can interact with
our component's HTML output with the associated JavaScript and styles included. As we
discussed in the *Selecting queries using the Testing Playground website* section, when we
click on the button, we get the preferred `getByRole` query selector. When we copy the
selector, we get the query code to add to our test:

```
screen.getByRole('button', { name: /more info/i})
```

In the preceding code, we copied the `getByRole` selector to access the **More Info** button.
Next, we will use the extension to help select the popover, which is displayed after clicking
on the button:

```
suggested query
> getByRole('heading', { name: /lorem ipsum/i })
```

Figure 6.25 – The popover query selector

In the preceding screenshot, `getByRole` is the suggested query for the `popover` element after selecting it in the browser. Now we have all the selectors that we need to write the remaining test code:

```
user.click(screen.getByRole('button', { name: /more info/i
   }))

const popover = await screen.findByRole('heading', { name: /
   lorem ipsum/i })


expect(popover).toBeInTheDocument()
```

In the preceding code, first, we click on the **More Info** button. Next, we grab the `popover` element by its heading and store it in a variable. Notice that we used `findByRole` instead of the `getByRole` query. Testing Playground only provides `getBy*` queries, so it might be necessary to modify the copied query based on the situation. Finally, we assert that the `popover` element is in the DOM. When we run the test, we get the following result:

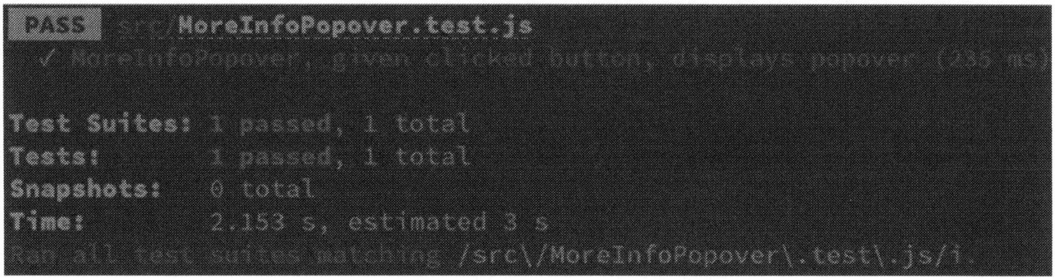

Figure 6.26 – The popover test results

In the previous screenshot, the results indicate that the `MoreInfoPopover, given clicked button, displays popover` test passes as expected. Now you know how to install and use the Testing Playground Chrome extension to enhance your workflow when writing tests. The Testing Playground website and extension are great supporting tools to utilize when working with DOM Testing Library.

In the next section, we will learn how to use a tool that will speed up the results feedback from beginning to completion when writing tests.

Increasing our testing productivity with Wallaby.js

In this section, we will learn how to increase our productivity by using the Wallaby.js productivity tool. Wallaby.js works by automatically running your tests behind the scenes via a Headless Chrome browser. There is also the option to run tests in other environments, such as Node.js or Phantom.js, with a custom configuration file. Wallaby.js helps to speed up your workflow by providing immediate test results inside your code editor, so you can type without needing to save and run a test script to view the results.

Wallaby.js provides many features, such as the following:

- **Time Travel Debugging**: This allows you to navigate through your code to pinpoint bug sources easily.

- **Test Story Viewer**: This provides the ability to view the code associated with your test on one compact screen.

- **Inline Code Coverage**: This informs you of the test coverage for each line of code inside the code editor.

> **Note**
>
> Please refer to the *Features* section (`https://wallabyjs.com/#features`) on the Wallaby.js documentation website for a complete list of features.

Installing and configuring Wallaby.js

In this section, we will learn how to install and set up Wallaby.js for the Visual Studio Code editor. Please refer to the *Install* section (`https://wallabyjs.com/download/`) on the Wallaby.js documentation website for a complete list of installation options. To get started, add the Wallaby.js VSCode extension to your editor via the *VSCode Marketplace* (`https://marketplace.visualstudio.com/items?itemName=WallabyJs.wallaby-vscode`). Once the extension has been installed, we can configure it to work in our project.

The quickest and easiest way to configure Wallaby.js is with automatic configuration. Projects using specific versions of tools such as `create-react-app version 3` or greater, or `Jest version 24` or greater, qualify for automatic configuration.

For projects that do not qualify for automatic configuration, please refer to the *Configuration File* section (`https://wallabyjs.com/docs/intro/config.html?editor=vsc#configuration-file`) in the Wallaby.js documentation for specific configurations based on your project setup.

Start Wallaby.js in VSCode with automatic configuration using the command palette:

Figure 6.27 – Select Configuration

In the preceding screenshot, `wallaby` is entered into the command palette to bring up the available Wallaby.js commands. We will click on the **Wallaby.js: Select Configuration** option:

> Automatic Configuration <project directory>
> Automatic Configuration <custom directory>...

Figure 6.28 – The Automatic Configuration option

In the preceding screenshot, we have selected the **Automatic Configuration <project directory>** and **Automatic Configuration <custom directory>** options. We will select **<project directory>** to use the directory of our current project. Once we select the configuration, Wallaby.js will start and run our tests to provide feedback directly inside the test files of the code editor, as shown in the following screenshot:

```
Debug | View story | Profile | Focus
it('logs output to Testing Playground', () => {       45ms
  render(<MoreInfoPopover />)
  screen.logTestingPlaygroundURL()
})
```

Figure 6.29 – Wallaby.js enhanced test output

In the preceding screenshot, we can see a test that we created earlier, in the *Selecting the best queries with Testing Playground* section of this chapter, enhanced with Wallaby.js' features. First, we see green-colored square shapes to the left of the line numbers indicating that all the test lines have passed. Next, we see links for the Wallaby.js **Debug**, **View Story**, **Profile**, and **Focus** features, which we can click on to analyze the test from the perspective of that particular feature.

Finally, we see the test runtime, 45ms, logged next to the test. Now you understand how to install and configure Wallaby.js. You should also understand the basic enhancements that Wallaby.js adds directly inside the test files.

In the next section, we will walk through how to write a test utilizing Wallaby.js's Interactive Test Output feature.

Writing tests with Interactive Test Output

In the *Selecting the best queries with Testing Playground* section of this chapter, we wrote the MoreInfoPopover, given clicked button, displays popover test for a MoreInfoPopover component. Let's walk through how to create the same test utilizing Wallaby.js.

First, we will render the component under test in the DOM and use the debug method to log the current state of the HTML output:

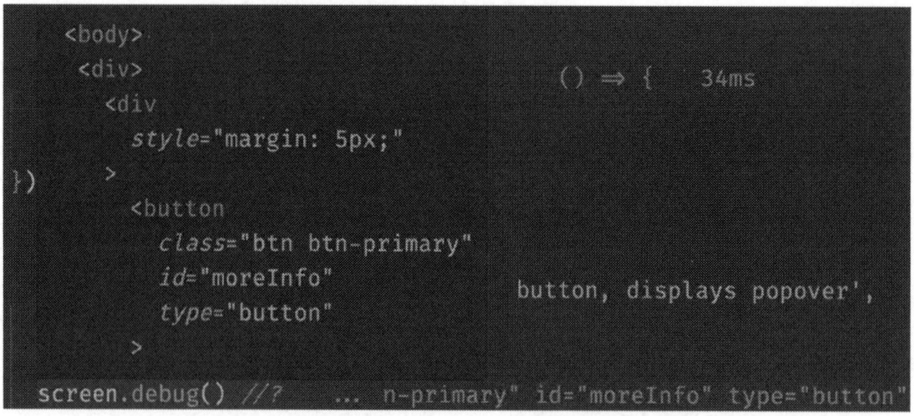

Figure 6.30 – The Wallaby.js inline debug output

In the preceding screenshot, we used the //? command from Wallaby.js to log the results of debug directly inside the code editor. The output is automatically displayed horizontally to the right of debug when we hover over the method. This feature speeds up our workflow because, normally, we would have to execute our test runner from the command line to see the output.

Next, we will add queries to select the DOM elements:

```
Unable to find an accessible element with the role "heading"
and name `/lorem ipsum/i`

Here are the accessible roles:

button:

Name "More Info":
<button
class="btn btn-primary"

test('MoreInfoPopover, given clicked button, displays popover',  () => {
    render(<MoreInfoPopover />)
        user.click(screen.getByRole('button', { name: /more info/i }))
        const popover = screen.getByRole('heading', { name: /lorem ipsum/i })
```

Figure 6.31 – A query error

In the preceding screenshot, we have a test failure resulting from React Testing Library not finding a `heading` element named `lorem ipsum`. Wallaby.js increases our ability to discover the error in two ways. First, we see a red-colored square shape to the left of the test name and, specifically, the line number where the error occurred. The inline code notifications help us to quickly identify where we should focus on pinpointing the cause of the error. Second, when we hover over the `test` method, React Testing Library's test result output is displayed directly in the code editor.

This feature speeds up our workflow because Wallaby.js reruns our test and provides feedback any time we add new code to the test. Furthermore, we don't even have to save our test file to gain feedback. We can also view test feedback in the **Wallaby.js Tests** console:

```
TERMINAL   PROBLEMS  6   OUTPUT   DEBUG CONSOLE                    Wallaby.js Tests       ∨   ≣   ⌂   ⤢   ∧
1 failing test, 5 passing  Launch Coverage & Test Explorer | Search Tests

  MoreInfoPopover, given clicked button, displays popover [95 ms] Debug test |
    Open test story

    TestingLibraryElementError: Unable to find an accessible element with the role "heading"
    and name `/lorem ipsum/i`

    Here are the accessible roles:
```

Figure 6.32 – The Wallaby.js Tests console

In the preceding screenshot, we can see similar React Testing Library feedback to what we see directly in the editor anytime code is updated in the test file, but now it is in an expanded view. Additionally, we can see the number of failing tests compared to passing tests, and clickable links for `Launch Coverage & Test Explorer`, which is a feature that allows you to see visualized test coverage for each file, and `Search Test`, which is a feature that allows you to quickly search for any test in the project.

After debugging the failure with the help of Wallaby.js' in-editor features, we learned that the `heading` element with the name of `lorem ipsum` is not immediately displayed. Using our knowledge of Testing Library queries, we can determine that the element should be selected using an asynchronous `findBy*` query:

```
const popover = await screen.findByRole('heading', { name: /
    lorem ipsum/i })
```

In the preceding code, we update the selector to `findByRole`. Immediately after updating the selector, we get feedback within the editor:

```
test('MoreInfoPopover, given clicked button, displays popover', async () => {
    render(<MoreInfoPopover />)
    user.click(screen.getByRole('button', { name: /more info/i }))
    const popover = await screen.findByRole('heading', { name: /lorem ipsum/i })

    expect(popover).toBeInTheDocument()
})
```

Figure 6.33 – Query refactor

In the preceding screenshot, we see green-colored square shapes to the left of all of the line numbers. This indicates that we have successfully refactored the test code to a working state. We have also written an assertion to verify that the test passes as expected. Now you know how to use Wallaby.js to gain instant editor feedback and test debugging capabilities. Using Wallaby.js is a great tool to have when you need to save time running and debugging tests.

Summary

This chapter has taught you the benefits of using ESLint plugins to follow the DOM Testing Library and `jest-dom` best practices. You have gained an understanding of accessible code and used `jest-axe` to increase the accessibility of your applications. You have learned how to speed up the process of determining the best query method with Testing Playground. Finally, you have learned how to increase test writing productivity with Wallaby.js.

In the next chapter, you will learn about end-to-end UI testing using the popular Cypress framework.

Questions

1. Install and configure the React-specific version of `eslint-plugin-testing-library` into a project and add additional rules.

2. Create examples of `jest` assertions using matchers that don't use `jest-dom` best practices. Then, install and configure `eslint-plugin-jest-dom` inside a project and use it as a guide to correct highlighted issues.

3. Create a few components with accessibility issues, install and run `jest-axe` against the components and use the feedback to fix them.

4. Visit three of your favorite websites and use Testing Playground to see how many elements you can select using DOM Testing Library's preferred `byRole*` queries.

5. Install Wallaby.js and log how quickly you can write a test using its in-editor features.

7
End-to-End UI Testing with Cypress

In previous chapters, we learned how to test applications at the component level using React Testing Library. In this chapter, we will learn how to test applications at the system level by executing end-to-end testing using Cypress. End-to-end tests play an essential role in helping teams gain the confidence their applications will work as expected for end users in production. By including end-to-end tests in test strategies, teams can gain a lot of knowledge about how applications behave when all dependencies work together. Cypress is a modern, JavaScript end-to-end testing framework that can handle anything that runs in the browser, including applications built with popular frameworks such as React, Angular, and Vue. Cypress features allow teams to install, write, run, and debug tests within minutes.

In addition to system-level testing, it provides the ability to write unit and integration tests, making the framework great for developers and quality engineers. Also, Cypress differs from tools such as Selenium by running tests directly in the browser versus requiring browser drivers, automatically waiting for commands and assertions before proceeding, providing visual feedback for each test command when run, and access to recorded test runs via the Cypress Dashboard.

In this chapter, we're going to cover the following main topics:

- Installing Cypress in an existing project
- Enhancing Cypress DOM queries with `cypress-testing-library`
- Using Cypress to implement test-driven development
- Reviewing Cypress design patterns
- Executing API testing with Cypress
- Implementing Gherkin-style tests with Cucumber

The knowledge gained in this chapter will add additional test strategies to complement skills learned with React Testing Library.

Technical requirements

For the examples in this chapter, you will need to have Node.js installed on your machine. We will be using the `create-react-app` CLI tool and the Next.js React framework (`https://nextjs.org/`) for all code examples. Please familiarize yourself with Next.js before starting the chapter if needed. Code snippets will be provided throughout the chapter to help you understand the code under test, but the objective is understanding how to test the code.

You can find code examples for this chapter here: `https://github.com/PacktPublishing/Simplify-Testing-with-React-Testing-Library/tree/master/Chapter07`.

Getting started with Cypress

In this section, you will learn how to install and set up **Cypress** in an existing project. We will also write a test for a user flow. Use the following command at the command line to install Cypress:

```
npm install cypress --save-dev
```

The preceding command will install Cypress as a development dependency in your project. Once Cypress is installed, run the following command:

```
npx cypress open
```

The preceding command runs the Cypress interactive Test Runner. The Test Runner allows us to manually do things such as select specific tests to run, pick a browser to use for test execution, and see the browser output alongside each associated Cypress command. When we run Cypress in interactive mode for the first time, it creates a suggested folder structure for Cypress projects:

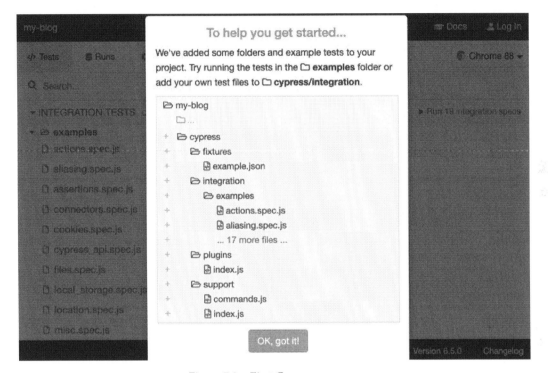

Figure 7.1 – First Cypress open run

In the preceding screenshot, Cypress informs us that it automatically created a cypress folder structure on our behalf in the root of the project that includes the following sub-folders – fixtures, integration, plugins, and support. The sub-folders allow us to quickly get up and running without needing to do any manual configuration. The fixtures folder is used to create static data typically used for stubbing network data in tests. The integration folder is used to create test files. Inside the integration folder, Cypress provides an examples folder with numerous examples of using Cypress to test applications.

The plugins folder is used to extend the behavior of Cypress in many ways, such as programmatically changing the config file, generating reports in HTML format after test runs, or adding support for automated visual testing, just to name a few. Cypress provides many *out-of-the-box* commands such as click, type, and assertions from third-party tools such as **Mocha** (https://mochajs.org/), **Chai** (https://www.chaijs.com/), and **jQuery** (https://jquery.com/).

The support folder is used to create custom commands or add third-party commands with tools such as **Cypress Testing Library**, which we will learn about in the next section, *Enhancing query selectors with Cypress Testing Library*. Cypress also creates a cypress.json file at the root of the project folder. The cypress.json file is used to set global settings such as the global base URL Cypress will use in tests, set custom timeouts for elements to appear in the DOM, or even change the folder location of our test files from integration to e2e, for example. There are numerous settings we can configure in the cypress.json file.

In the top-right corner of the Cypress Test Runner is a drop-down list allowing you to select the browser to use for test runs:

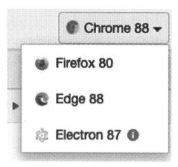

Figure 7.2 – Cypress browser dropdown

In the preceding screenshot, the **Chrome 88**, **Firefox 80**, **Edge 88**, and **Electron 87** version browsers are available to use for test runs. Available browsers are based on Cypress-compatible browsers installed on the user's machine. The Cypress-supported browsers are Firefox and Chrome-family browsers such as Edge and Electron. The Electron browser is available by default in Cypress and is also used for running tests in headless mode, meaning without the browser UI.

To execute a test, simply click the test name from the list of available tests:

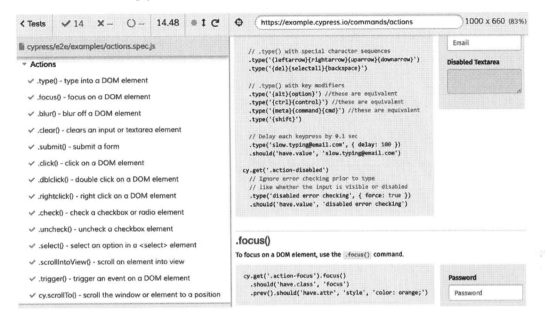

Figure 7.3 – Example test run

In the preceding screenshot, the `actions.spec.js` test file located in the `examples` folder was run. The screen's right side displays the state of the application in the browser throughout each step of the test. The left side of the screen shows the result of each test within the test file. If we wanted to, we could click into each test, hover over each Cypress command, and see the resulting DOM state before and after the command was executed. Being able to hover over each command to view the resulting DOM output is a great feature.

Cypress makes debugging easier as compared to other end-to-end testing frameworks. For example, if Cypress cannot find an element in the browser specified in our test, it provides helpful error messages:

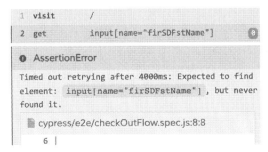

Figure 7.4 – Cypress error output

In the preceding screenshot, Cypress provides feedback by informing us that an input element named `firSDFstName` was never found after 4 seconds inside the Test Runner. Cypress also allows us to click a link to open our code editor at the line where the error occurred.

Now that we understand the basics of installing, running, and executing tests with the Cypress Test Runner, we will write a checkout flow test next. When a user checks out, the application progresses through four screens. The first screen is for the shipping address:

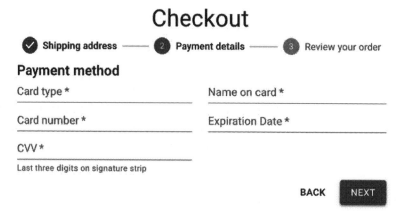

Figure 7.5 – Shipping address Checkout screen

In the preceding screenshot, a form is shown where a user can enter their shipping address information. The second screen is for the payment details:

Checkout

✓ **Shipping address** ──── ② **Payment details** ──── ③ Review your order

Payment method

Card type *   Name on card *

Card number *   Expiration Date *

CVV *

Last three digits on signature strip

BACK   NEXT

Figure 7.6 – Payment details Checkout screen

In the preceding screenshot, a form is shown where a user can enter their payment information. The third screen is for reviewing the order:

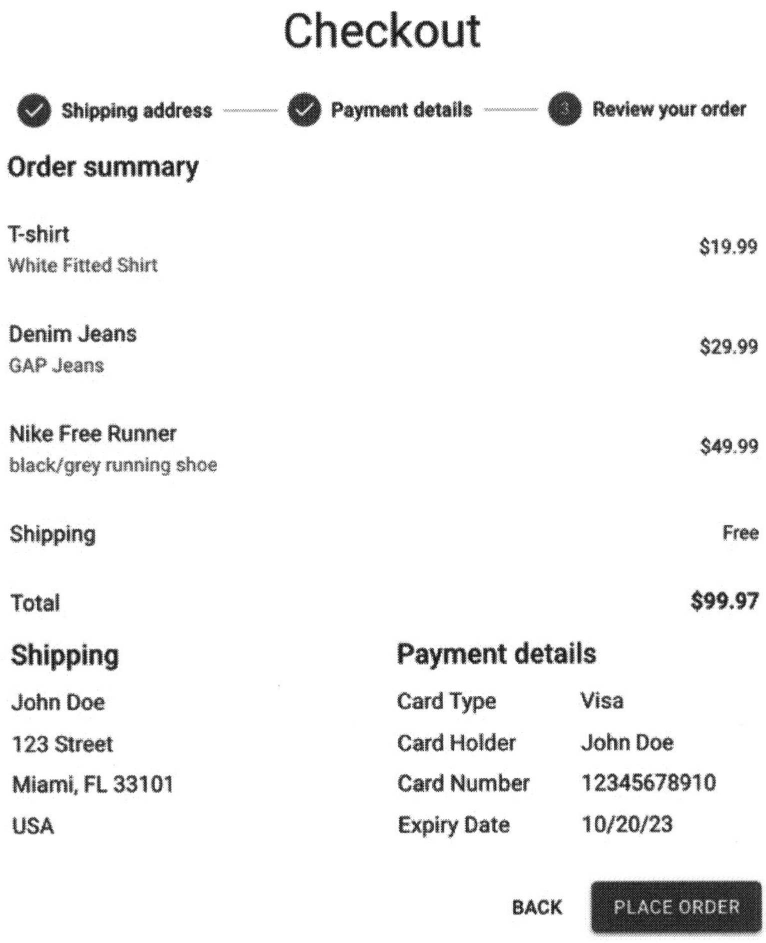

Checkout

✓ Shipping address ——— ✓ Payment details ——— ③ Review your order

Order summary

T-shirt White Fitted Shirt	$19.99
Denim Jeans GAP Jeans	$29.99
Nike Free Runner black/grey running shoe	$49.99
Shipping	Free
Total	**$99.97**

Shipping

John Doe

123 Street

Miami, FL 33101

USA

Payment details

Card Type	Visa
Card Holder	John Doe
Card Number	12345678910
Expiry Date	10/20/23

BACK   PLACE ORDER

Figure 7.7 – Review your order Checkout screen

In the preceding screenshot, a summary displaying all form values entered on previous screens is shown. Note, for the purposes of this demonstration, the purchased items **T-shirt**, **Denim Jeans**, and **Nike Free Runner** are hardcoded in the application and will not be a focus in the test we will write. The last screen is the order submitted screen:

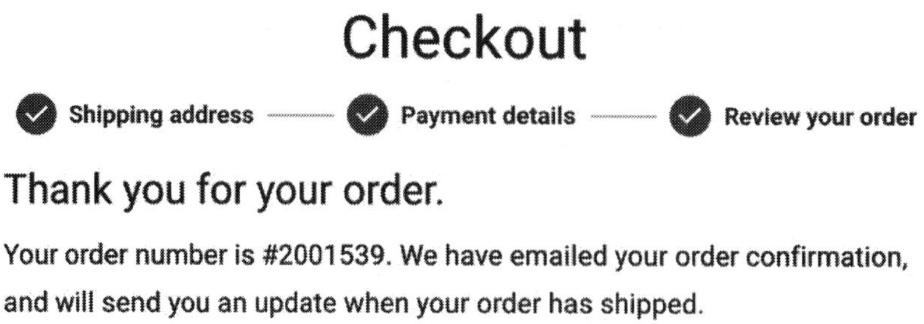

Checkout

Thank you for your order.

Your order number is #2001539. We have emailed your order confirmation,

and will send you an update when your order has shipped.

Figure 7.8 – Order submitted Checkout screen

In the preceding screenshot, a confirmation is shown, displaying a **Thank you** message, an order number, and information informing the customer about email communication for order updates.

For the purposes of this demonstration, the order number is hardcoded and will not be a focus of our test. Now that we understand the user flow, we can write the test code:

```
import user from '../support/user'

describe('Checkout Flow', () => {
  it('allows a user to enter address and payment info and place
      an order', () => {
    cy.visit('/')
```

In the preceding code, we first import a `user` object to use in the test. The `user` object simply provides fake values to enter into each `form` input, so we don't have to hardcode each value. Next, we use the `visit` command via the global `cy` variable to visit the application.

All available Cypress methods are chained off the `cy` variable. Note that the `'/'` used in the `visit` method represents the URL relative to our tests' base URL. By using a relative URL, we don't have to enter the full URL in our tests. We can set the `baseURL` property via the `cypress.json` file:

```
{
  "baseUrl": "http://localhost:3000"
}
```

In the preceding code, we set `baseUrl` to `http://localhost:3000`, allowing us to use `'/'` when we want to visit the index page or other pages relative to the index page.

Next, we will write the code to complete the **Shipping address** screen:

```
cy.get('input[name="firstName"]').type(user.firstName)
cy.get('input[name="lastName"]').type(user.lastName)
cy.get('input[name="address1"]').type(user.address1)
cy.get('input[name="city"]').type(user.city)
cy.get('input[name="state"]').type(user.state)
cy.get('input[name="zipCode"]').type(user.zipCode)
cy.get('input[name="country"]').type(user.country)
cy.contains(/next/i).click()
```

In the preceding code, we use the `get` command to select each input element via its `name` attribute. We also use the `type` command to enter a value for each input. Next. We use the `contains` command to select the button element with the text `next` and click it using the `click` command.

Next, we will enter values for the **Payment details** screen:

```
cy.get('input[name="cardType"]').type(user.cardType)
cy.get('input[name="cardHolder"]').type(user.cardHolder)
cy.get('input[name="cardNumber"]').type(user.cardNumber)
cy.get('input[name="expiryDate"]').type(user.expiryDate)
cy.get('input[name="cardCvv"]').type(user.cardCvv)
cy.contains(/next/i).click()
```

In the preceding code, we use the `get` and `type` commands to select and enter values in each input. Then, we use the `contains` command to click the **next** button.

Next, we will verify entered values for shipping and payment details on the **Review your order** screen:

```
cy.contains(`${user.firstName}
  ${user.lastName}`).should('be.visible')
cy.contains(user.address1).should('be.visible')
cy.contains(`${user.city}, ${user.state}
  ${user.zipCode}`).should(
    'be.visible'
  )
```

```
cy.contains(user.country).should('be.visible')
cy.contains(user.cardType).should('be.visible')
cy.contains(user.cardHolder).should('be.visible')
cy.contains(user.cardNumber).should('be.visible')
cy.contains(user.expiryDate).should('be.visible')
cy.contains(/place order/i).click()
```

We use the contains command to select each element via form values entered on previous screens in the preceding code. We also use the should command to assert that each element is visible on the screen. Then, we use the contains command to select the button with the text place order and click it using the click command.

Finally, we verify the application lands on the order submitted screen:

```
cy.contains(/thank you for your
    order/i).should('be.visible')
```

In the preceding code, we use the contains and should commands to verify an element with the text **Thank you for your order.** visible on the screen. To run the test, we can use the npx cypress open command directly at the command line as previously learned at the beginning of this section, but we can also create an npm script:

```
"cy:open": "cypress open",
```

In the preceding code, we create a cy:open script to run the Cypress Test Runner. We can also create another script to run tests in headless mode:

```
"cy:run": "cypress run",
```

We create a cy:run script to run Cypress in headless mode via the cypress run command in the preceding code. We can use the cy:run script in situations where we don't want to use the interactive mode, such as running via a **Continuous Integration and Continuous Delivery (CI/CD)** server. Before running Cypress, be sure that your development server is already up and running because Cypress does not start the development server for you. When we execute the test via the cy:open interactive mode, we get the following output:

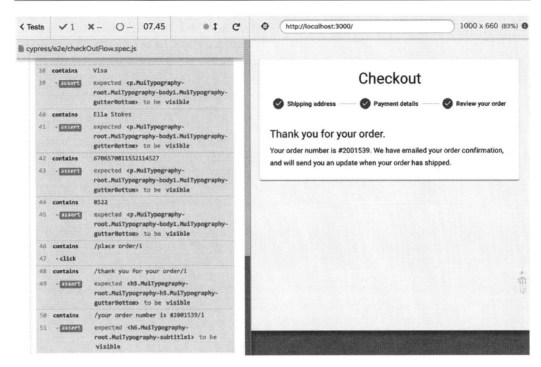

Figure 7.9 – Checkout flow test results

In the previous screenshot, the test run indicates the checkOutFlow test passed as expected. Now you know how to install and use Cypress to test a user flow. In the next section, we will install a plugin to enhance our element selector commands.

Enhancing Cypress commands with the Cypress Testing Library

In the previous section, we learned how to install and write a user flow test using Cypress. In this section, we will learn how to install and configure the **Cypress Testing Library** to add enhanced query selectors. The Cypress Testing Library will allow us to use DOM Testing Library query methods in Cypress. Install the library using the following command:

```
npm install --save-dev @testing-library/cypress
```

The preceding code installs @testing-library/cypress as a development dependency in your project. After the library is installed, we can add it to the Cypress commands file:

```
import '@testing-library/cypress/add-commands'
```

In the preceding code, we extended the Cypress commands with those from the Cypress Testing Library. Now that we have the Cypress Testing Library installed, we can use it in our tests. It should be noted that only findBy* methods from the DOM Testing Library are included to support the Cypress retry-ability feature that retries commands a number of times before timing out.

In the *Getting started with Cypress* section of this chapter, we wrote a test for a checkout flow. We can refactor element queries in that test with those from the Cypress Testing Library. For example, we can refactor the code for the **Shipping address** screen like so:

```
cy.findByRole('textbox', { name: /first name/i
}).type(user.firstName)
cy.findByRole('textbox', { name: /last name/i
}).type(user.lastName)
cy.findByRole('textbox', { name: /address line 1/i
}).type(user.address1)
cy.findByRole('textbox', { name: /city/i
}).type(user.city)
cy.findByRole('textbox', { name: /state/i
}).type(user.state)
cy.findByRole('textbox', { name: /postal code/i
}).type(user.zipCode)
cy.findByRole('textbox', { name: /country/i
}).type(user.country)
cy.findByText(/next/i).click()
```

In the previous code, we updated all selectors to find `input` elements by their **Accessible Rich Internet Application (ARIA)** textbox role using `findByRole` queries. ARIA attributes are used by individuals using assistive technology to locate elements. We also updated the selector for the **next** button by using the `findByText` query. The same refactoring pattern is used for the **Payment details** and **Review your order** screens. Finally, we can refactor the code for the order submitted screen like so:

```
cy.findByRole('heading', { name: /thank you for
    your order/i }).should(
  'be.visible'
)
cy.findByRole('heading', { name: /your order number is
  #2001539/i }).should(
  'be.visible'
)
```

In the previous code, we updated the two selectors to find elements by their heading role using the `findByRole` query. Our test code now queries elements in ways that are more accessible, providing more confidence that the application will work for all users, including those using assistive technology such as screen readers. Also, the test code reads better when viewing each line in the Test Runner screen.

Now you know how to install the Cypress Testing Library and refactor existing tests using queries that avoid using implementation details. In the next section, we will learn how to use test-driven development with Cypress to add features to a blog application.

Cypress-driven development

In the previous section, we installed the Cypress Testing Library and refactored an existing test for a checkout flow. In this section, we will use Cypress to drive the development of new features for an existing blog application created with **Next.js**. Next.js is a popular framework that provides a pleasant experience for teams to build static or server-rendered React applications.

Example features that Next.js provides are *out-of-the-box* routing, built-in CSS support, and API routes. Please see the Next.js documentation (`https://nextjs.org/`) for more details. The **MY BLOG** application currently has two pages, a **Home** page displaying all blog posts and a page to display blog details. The page that displays a list of posts looks as follows:

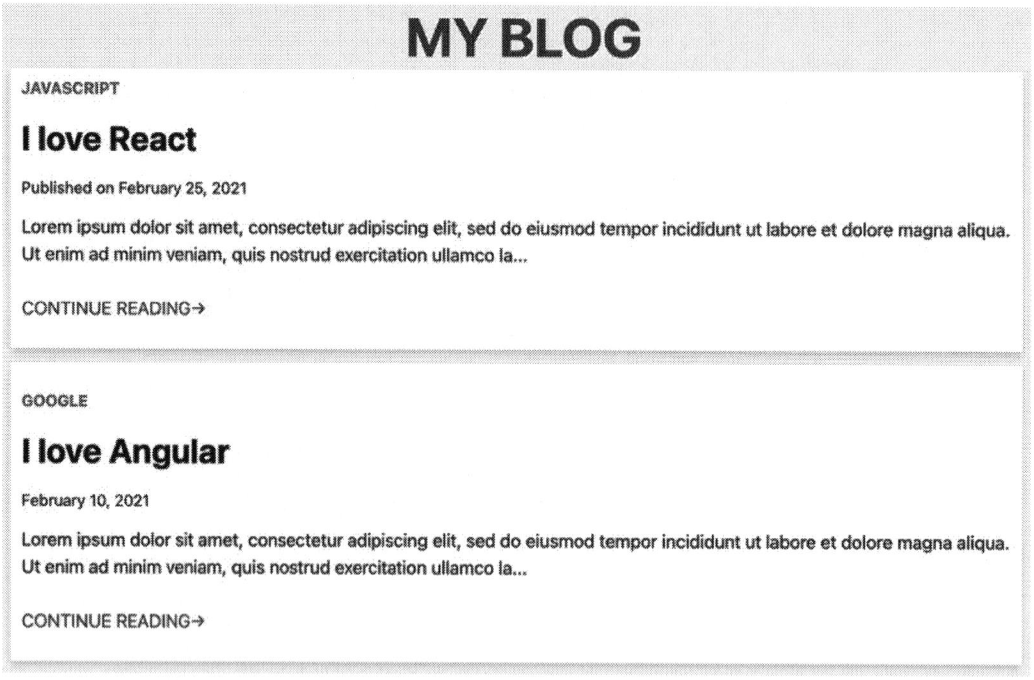

Figure 7.10 – Blog home page

In the previous screenshot, the **Home** page displays two blog posts, **I love React** and **I love Angular**. Blog data is stored in a MongoDB database and sent to the frontend via the API once the application loads. Each blog post displays a category, title, published date, an excerpt, and a **Continue Reading** link from top to bottom.

To view a blog's details, a user can click either the blog title or the **Continue Reading** link. For example, we see the following after clicking the **I love React** title:

Figure 7.11 – Blog detail page

We see the full content of the **I love React** blog post in the preceding screenshot. We also see the published date and a **BACK TO BLOG** link to navigate back to the **Home** page. The application's current state only allows new blog posts to be created via a POST request to the API or directly adding new posts to the database.

We need to add a feature that allows users to add new posts via the UI. We can use Cypress to write a test for the expected behavior and build out the UI little by little until the feature is complete and the test passes. The following test shows the final expected behavior:

```
import fakePost from '../support/generateBlogPost'


describe('Blog Flow', () => {
    let post = {}
  beforeEach(()=> (post = fakePost()))
  it('allows a user to create a new blog post', () => {
    cy.visit('/')
    cy.findByRole('link', { name: /new post/i }).click()
```

In the previous code, first, we import `fakePost`, a custom method that will generate unique test data for each test run and set it as the value for the variable post. We don't want to create identical blog posts, so the custom method helps by always creating unique data. Next, we visit the **Home** page and click a link with the name **New Post**. The **New Post** link should navigate us to a page where we can enter values for a new post.

Next, we test the code for entering values for the new post:

```
cy.findByRole('textbox', { name: /title/i
    }).type(post.title)
cy.findByRole('textbox', { name: /category/i
    }).type(post.category)
cy.findByRole('textbox', { name: /image link/i
    }).type(post.image_url)
cy.findByRole('textbox', { name: /content/i
    }).type(post.content)
```

In the preceding code, we find each `textbox` element by its unique name and enter associated values via the custom `post` method. Finally, we create the last pieces of the test:

```
cy.findByRole('button', { name: /submit/i }).click()
cy.findByRole('link', { name: post.title
    }).should('be.visible')
})
})
```

In the preceding code, we click the **submit** button. Once we click the **submit** button, the data should be sent to the API, saved to the database, and then the application should navigate us back to the **Home** page. Finally, once on the **Home** page, we verify the title for the post we created is visible on the screen.

We will run the test using the Cypress Test Runner to utilize its interactive features and keep it open throughout building the feature. Our test will fail as expected when run:

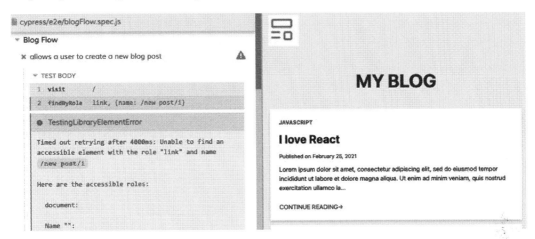

Figure 7.12 – Blog Flow test failure

In the previous screenshot, the first step succeeded in navigating to the **Home** page, but the output informs us that the test failed because a `link` element with the name **New Post** was not found after 4 seconds in the second test step. Four seconds is the default time that Cypress will continue to query for the element before timing out.

We also see a helpful message from the DOM Testing Library informing us which accessible elements are visible in the DOM. Further, we can look at the browser at the point of test failure and see that the **New Post** link is not visible. Now we can update the UI to make the second test step pass:

```
<Link href="/add">
<a className="font-bold inline-block px-4 py-2 text-3xl">
   New Post
</a>
</Link>
```

In the previous code, we added a link that will navigate the user to an **Add a new blog** page when clicked. Notice the `hyperlink` element is wrapped in a `Link` component. The `Link` component allows for client-side route navigation. The Test Runner automatically reruns when we save the test file. Since we already wrote all the necessary test code, we can trigger a test run by saving the file.

We will need to perform this action after each UI change. Now we get the following output when the test runs:

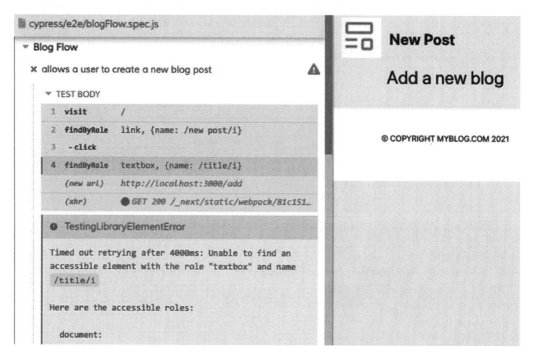

Figure 7.13 – Blog Flow add page failure

In the previous screenshot, our test code can now successfully open the **Home** page, click the **New Post** link and land on the **Add** page. However, now the output indicates our test failed because an element with the name `title` and role `textbox` was not found at step **4**. We can update the UI by creating an `input` element with the name `title` and the `textbox` role:

```
<label htmlFor="title">Title</label>
 <input
   type="text"
   autoFocus
   id="title"
   name="title"
   placeholder="Blog Title"
   value={newBlog.title}
   onChange={handleChange}
 />
```

In the previous code, we add a `Title label` element and an associated `input` element of type `text`. Although not demonstrated in the last code, we also went ahead and added the `Category`, `Image link`, and `Content` input elements similar in structure to the `Title input` element. Now we get the following output when we trigger a test run:

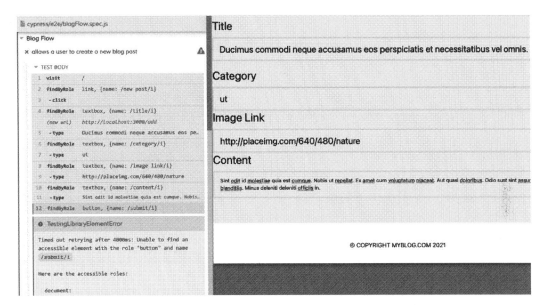

Figure 7.14 – Blog Flow add page input element refactor

In the previous screenshot, our test code can now successfully open the **Home** page. Click the **New Post** link, and add values in the `Title`, `Category`, `Image link`, and `Content input` elements on the **Add** page. However, now the output indicates our test failed because a `Submit` button was not found at step **12**. We can update the UI by creating the `Submit` button:

```
<button>Submit</button>
```

We created and added a Submit button to the **Add** page in the previous code. The Submit button is part of the form element and, when clicked, calls a method that sends the form data to the API and, ultimately, the database. Although not a focus for our test, we also added a cancel button element in the UI. Now we get the following output when we trigger a test run:

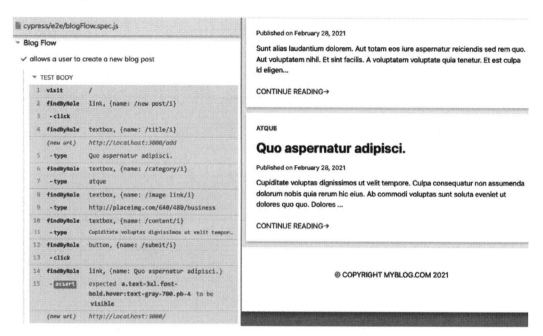

Figure 7.15 – Blog Flow add page completed refactor

In the previous screenshot, the output indicates the test finally passes. We can see the new blog post in the browser created by our test on the screen's right side. With the last refactor, we have completed all the feature steps that allow users to add new posts via the UI.

For our next feature, we want users to have the ability to delete blog posts via the UI. We will add a `delete` link to the blog detail page that makes a DELETE request to the API when clicked. The application's current state only allows blog posts to be deleted via a DELETE request to the API or directly in the database. Our previous test can be updated to perform actions to delete the new blog post after creation like so:

```
cy.findByRole('link', { name: post.title }).click()
cy.findByText(/delete post>/i).click()
cy.findByRole('link', { name: post.title
   }).should('not.exist')
```

In the preceding code, first, we click the title of the blog post to delete to navigate to its detail page. Next, we find and click the link with the text `delete post`. Finally, we verify the post is no longer in the list of blog posts on the **Home** page. We get the following output when we trigger a test run by saving the file:

Figure 7.16 – Blog Flow delete post test failure

In the previous screenshot, the output indicates the test failed at step **18** when an element with the text `delete post` could not be found. We can update the UI by creating the missing element:

```
<a onClick={handleDelete}>Delete post&#62;</a>;
```

In the preceding code, we add a `hyperlink` element with the text `Delete post`. When the hyperlink is clicked, it calls a `handleDelete` method to send a `DELETE` request to the API and ultimately remove the blog post from the database. We get the following output when we save the test file to trigger a test run:

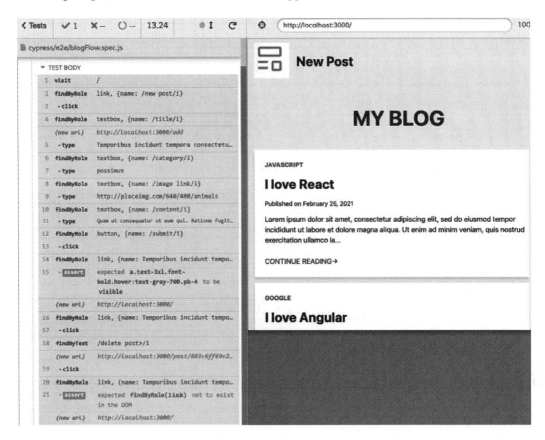

Figure 7.17 – Blog Flow delete post completed refactor

In the previous screenshot, the output indicates the test finally passes with the blog post deleted. With the addition of the `delete` link, we have completed all the feature steps that allow users to delete blog posts via the UI. Now you know how to develop features using Cypress-driven development.

The approach can be beneficial when you want to see the application in a specific state as you build out a feature. In the next section, we will cover Cypress design patterns.

Writing Tests using Cypress design patterns

In the previous section, we learned how to use Cypress to drive the development of new features to a blog application. In this section, we will look at two design patterns to structure our Cypress code. Design patterns help teams by providing solutions to problems such as writing maintainable code or designing responsive websites. First, we will look at the Page Object Model, followed by custom commands.

Creating page objects in Cypress

The **Page Object Model** (**POM**) is a popular design pattern commonly used in Selenium test frameworks to increase readability and maintainability for end-to-end tests. The POM model consists of creating an object-oriented `class` representation for each page in an application, including custom methods to select and interact with various page elements. An advantage of using the POM model is abstracting away multiple lines of test code inside a single method.

Also, page objects serve as a single source of truth for actions performed on specific pages. In the *Cypress-driven development* section, we added a feature to allow users to create a new blog post through the UI. We can refactor the test code using the POM pattern. First, we will create a page object for the **Home** page:

```
class HomePage {
  navigateToHomePage() {
    cy.visit('/')
  }
  navigateToAddPage() {
    cy.findByRole('link', { name: /new post/i }).click()
  }
  getBlogPost(post) {
    return cy.findByRole('link', { name: post.title })
  }
}
export const homePage = new HomePage()
```

In the preceding code, first, we create a page object for the **Home** page with `navigateToHomePage`, `navigateToAddPage`, and `getBlogPost` methods. Then, we export a new instance of the object to use in test files. Next, we will create a page object for the **Add** page:

```
class AddPage {
  createNewPost(newPost) {
    cy.findByRole('textbox', { name: /title/i
      }).type(newPost.title)
    cy.findByRole('textbox', { name: /category/i
      }).type(newPost.category)
    cy.findByRole('textbox', { name: /image link/i
      }).type(newPost.image_url)
    cy.findByRole('textbox', { name: /content/i
      }).type(newPost.content)
    cy.findByRole('button', { name: /submit/i }).click()
  }
}
export const addPage = new AddPage()
```

In the preceding code, we create a page object for the **Add** page with a `createNewPost` method that accepts a `newPost` object with data to enter for the new post. The page object is exported for use in test files. Now that we have page objects representing the **Home** and **Add** pages, we can use them in a test:

```
import post from '../support/generateBlogPost'
import { addPage } from './pages/AddPage'
import { homePage } from './pages/HomePage'
```

In the preceding code, first, we import the fake `post` method to generate unique post data in the test. Next, we import the `addPage` and `homePage` page objects. Next, we will write the main test code:

```
it('POM: allows a user to create a new blog post', ()
=> {
homePage.navigateToHomePage()
homePage.navigateToAddPage()
addPage.createNewPost(post)
homePage.getBlogPost(post).should('be.visible')
})
```

In the preceding code, first, we navigate to the **Home** page. Next, we navigate to the **Add** page. Then, we create a new post with values from the fake `post` method. Finally, we get the new post on the **Home** page and verify that it is visible on the screen.

In the *Cypress-driven development* section, we added another feature to delete blog posts through the UI. We can add a method for this feature in our page objects and verify our test's behavior. First, we will add a new method to the `homePage` page object:

```
navigateToPostDetail(post) {
  cy.findByRole('link', { name: post.title }).click()
}
```

In the previous code, we added a `navigateToPostDetail` method that accepts a `post` argument when called. Next, we will create a page object for the **Post Detail** page:

```
class PostDetailPage {
  deletePost() {
    cy.findByText(/delete post>/i).click()
  }
}
export const postDetailPage = new PostDetailPage()
```

In the preceding code, we created a page object for the **Post Detail** page and added a `deletePost` method. We also exported an instance of the page object to use in tests. Now we can use the new page object methods in our existing test:

```
import { postDetailPage } from './pages/PostDetailPage'
```

In the previous code, first, we import the `postDetailPage` page object similar to how we did with other page objects. Next, we will add the associated methods to delete the post:

```
homePage.navigateToPostDetail(post)
postDetailPage.deletePost()
homePage.getBlogPost(post).should('not.exist')
```

In the preceding code, we invoked the `navigateToPostDetail` and `deletePost` methods and verified the post no longer exists on the **Home** page. Now our task of refactoring the test code to page objects is completed. Our test code is shorter and abstracts away many test step details.

However, our page object design does present an issue if we split the *add blog post* and *delete blog post* features into two different tests. The first test will create a blog post:

```
it('POM: allows a user to create a new blog post', () => {
  homePage.navigateToHomePage()
  homePage.navigateToAddPage()
  addPage.createNewPost(post)
  homePage.getBlogPost(post).should('be.visible')
})
```

In the preceding code, the test `'POM: allows a user to create a new blog post'` creates a blog post. Next, we will create the test to delete the blog post:

```
it('POM: allows a user to delete a new blog post', () => {
  homePage.navigateToHomePage()
  homePage.navigateToAddPage()
  addPage.createNewPost(post)
  homePage.navigateToPostDetail(post)
  postDetailPage.deletePost()
  homePage.getBlogPost(post).should('not.exist')
})
```

In the preceding code, the test `'POM: allows a user to delete a new blog post'` deletes a blog post. The **Delete** test's problem is that we have to write many of the same test steps from the previous test and the actions most important to the test to delete the post. As a testing best practice, we want to avoid writing the same test steps in multiple tests.

In the next section, we will learn how to resolve this problem with custom Cypress commands.

Creating custom Commands in Cypress

In the previous section, we learned how to write tests using the POM pattern. However, we came across an issue where we had to write the same test steps in a different test. Cypress provides a custom command feature to resolve the issue. Custom commands allow us to add additional commands to Cypress. In the *Enhancing Cypress commands with the Cypress Testing Library* section, we added third-party custom commands. Now we will learn how to write our own custom commands. First, we will create a custom method to create a new blog post:

```
Cypress.Commands.add('createBlogPost', post => {
  cy.visit('/')
  cy.findByRole('link', { name: /new post/i }).click()
  cy.findByRole('textbox', { name: /title/i
  }).type(post.title)
  cy.findByRole('textbox', { name: /category/i
  }).type(post.category)
  cy.findByRole('textbox', { name: /image link/i
  }).type(post.image_url)
  cy.findByRole('textbox', { name: /content/i
  }).type(post.content)
  cy.findByRole('button', { name: /submit/i }).click()
})
```

In the preceding code, we add a custom `createBlogPost` command to Cypress via the `Commands.add` method inside the `commands.js` file. Next, we will use the custom method in our test:

```
it('Custom Command: allows a user to delete a new blog
  post', () => {
  cy.createBlogPost(post)
  homePage.navigateToPostDetail(post)
  postDetailPage.deletePost()
  homePage.getBlogPost(post).should('not.exist')
})
```

In the preceding code, we replace the previous code that creates a new blog post with the custom `createBlogPost` method we created. The custom method eliminates the need to explicitly write the same code lines to create a blog post. We can use the custom method in any future test when needed. However, for our specific test to delete a blog post, we can go a step further.

Although our custom `createBlogPost` method eliminates the need to write duplicate lines of code, we are still performing the same steps to create a new blog post via the UI. Executing the same steps in multiple tests is a bad testing practice as we are repeating steps we've already tested. If we have controllable access to our application's API, we can reduce repeated steps through the UI.

Cypress provides an HTTP `request client` that we can use to communicate with the API directly. Using the `request client`, we can bypass the UI to avoid repeating steps already tested and speed up our test. We can refactor our custom `createBlogPost` method like so:

```
cy.request('POST', '/api/add', post).then(response => {
    expect(response.body.message).to.equal(
      `The blog "${post.title}" was successfully added`
    )
})
```

In the previous code, we use the `request` method to make a `POST` request to the API at `/api/add` and send a `post` object containing values for the new post. Then we assert the server sends back the message `The blog "blog title here" was successfully added`, indicating the new post was added to the database. Note that `"blog title here"` in the message would be replaced with the blog post's real title when the request is made. Now we can update our test code:

```
cy.createBlogPost(post)
homePage.navigateToHomePage()
homePage.navigateToPostDetail(post)
postDetailPage.deletePost()
homePage.getBlogPost(post).should('not.exist')
```

In the previous code, our test looks almost identical to the previous version. The only change is the implementation of the `createBlogPost` method and adding the `navigateToHomePage` method. However, now the test will run faster because we skip creating a new blog post through the UI. Although we used the POM pattern along with custom commands in this section, it should be noted that we could have solely used custom commands.

We only need to test the *add blog post* and *delete blog post* features in one unique test to add the confidence they will work as expected for users. If tagged as critical user flows, the tests could run again in regression test suites to ensure the features continue to work as new features are added. We could write the Cypress commands to interact with the application directly without using the POM pattern and use custom commands in situations where we have to rerun the same steps.

Now you know how to structure maintainable test code and reduce duplicate steps by implementing the POM pattern and custom Cypress commands.

In the next section, we will build our knowledge of the Cypress `request client` by testing our application's API routes.

Testing APIs with Cypress

In the previous section, we learned how to structure test code using the POM and custom commands design patterns. We also learned that we could use Cypress to interact with our application's API directly. In this section, we will build on the previous section's learnings by testing the API of the blog application previously introduced in the *Cypress-driven development* section.

The blog application accepts four API requests: a GET request to get all posts, a POST request to add a post, a POST request to get a single post, and a DELETE request to delete a post. First, we will test the GET request for all posts:

```
import fakePost from '../support/generateBlogPost';
  const post = fakePost()


const getAllPosts = () => cy.request('/api/posts').its('body.
posts');
const deletePost = (post) =>
  cy.request('DELETE', `/api/delete/${post.id}`, {
    id: post.id,
    name: post.title,
```

```
  });

const deleteAllPosts = () => getAllPosts().each(deletePost);
beforeEach(deleteAllPosts);
```

In the preceding code, first, we import the `fakePost` method used to generate dynamic post data for each test run and assign it to the variable post. Next, we create three test setup methods: `getAllPosts`, `deletePost`, and `deleteAllPosts`. Before each test run, we want to start with an empty database.

The `deleteAllPosts` method will get all current posts from the database via `getAllPosts`, which calls `deletePost` to delete each post. Finally, we pass `deleteAllPosts` to `beforeEach`, which will call `deleteAllPosts` before each test run. Next, we will write the main code for the *get all posts* request:

```
cy.request('POST', '/api/add', {
    title: post.title,
    category: post.category,
    image_url: post.image_url,
    content: post.content
})

cy.request('/api/posts').as('posts')
cy.get('@posts').its('status').should('equal', 200)
cy.get('@posts').its('body.posts.length').should('equal',
1)
```

In the preceding code, we first use the `request` method to add a new blog post to the API to save in the database. Next, we use `request` to get all posts from the database. Since we wiped the database before the test, we should receive the one blog post we just created from the database.

We use the `as` method, a Cypress feature that allows us to save a code line as an alias. Then, we use the `get` method to access the alias using the required @ symbol before the alias name to verify the API server's response status code is `200`. Finally, we assert that the length of the `posts` body is `1`. Next, we will test the *create new blog post* request:

```
cy.request('POST', '/api/add', post).as('newPost')
cy.get('@newPost').its('status').should('equal', 200)
cy.get('@newPost')
  .its('body.message')
  .should('be.equal', `The blog "${post.title}" was
    successfully added`)
```

In the preceding code, first, we created a new blog post and saved the result as an alias labeled `newPost`. Then, we verify the API response status is `200` and that the response message is `The blog "title here" was successfully added`, where `"title here"` would be equal to the actual title in the test. Next, we will test the *delete a post* request:

```
cy.request('POST', '/api/add', post)

getAllPosts().each(post =>
  cy
    .request('DELETE', `/api/delete/${post.id}`, {
      id: post.id,
      title: post.title
    })
    .then(response => {
      expect(response.status).equal(200)
      expect(response.body.message).equal(
        `post "${post.title}" successfully deleted`
      )
    })
)
```

In the preceding code, we add a new post similar to what we did in previous tests. Then, we use `getAllPosts` to requests all current posts, which is only one, and make a `DELETE` request to remove each one from the application. Then, we verify the API sends a status of 200 indicating successful deletion.

Finally, we verify the API sends a response message that provides textual confirmation that the post has been deleted. For the final test, we will verify the *get a single post* request:

```
cy.request('POST', '/api/add', post)


getAllPosts().each(post =>
  cy
    .request(`/api/post/${post.id}`)
    .its('body.post.title')
    .should('equal', post.title)
  )
})
```

In the preceding code, first, we create a new post similar to previous tests. Then, we get all posts and verify the post `title` sent back from the API matches the `title` of the created post. Now you know how to test APIs using Cypress. It is great knowing that Cypress provides features to perform end-to-end testing for the API and UI, all in the same framework.

In the next section, we will learn how to create Gherkin-style test scenarios using Cucumber.

Writing Gherkin-style tests with Cucumber

In the previous section, we learned how to use Cypress to test API responses. In this section, we will learn how to create Gherkin-style tests with **Cucumber**. **Gherkin** is a behavior-driven development language used by Cucumber to describe test scenarios' behavior in a *plain-English* format. Tests written in Gherkin also make it easier for software teams to communicate and provide context for test cases with business leaders.

Gherkin uses the following keywords: `Feature`, `Scenario`, `Given`, `When`, and `Then`. `Feature` is used to describe the thing to build, such as a login page, for example. `Scenario` describes the user flow for the feature. For example, a user can enter a username, password, and click **Login** to navigate to their profile page.

The `Given`, `When`, and `Then` keywords describe the scenario at different stages. We could write a complete Gherkin test for a login feature like so:

```
Feature: Login


    Scenario: A user can enter a username, password, and
```

```
click login to navigate to their profile page.
Given I am on the login page
When I enter a username
When I enter a password
When I click "login"
Then I am navigated to my profile page
```

In the previous code, we created a Gherkin test for a login feature. We can use the `cypress-cucumber-preprocessor` plugin to write Gherkin-style tests using Cypress. Install the plugin using the following command:

```
npm install --save-dev cypress-cucumber-preprocessor
```

The previous command installs the `cucumber` plugin as a development dependency in your project. Once the plugin is installed, we can configure it for use in our Cypress project:

```
const cucumber = require('cypress-cucumber-
  preprocessor').default
module.exports = (on, config) => {
  on('file:preprocessor', cucumber())
}
```

In the preceding code, we add the `cucumber` plugin to the Cypress plugins file. Now the `cucumber` plugin features can be used in our tests. Next, we will add the plugin's `feature` file type to our global configuration file:

```
{
  "testFiles": "**/*.feature"
}
```

In the preceding code, we configure Cypress to use files with the `feature` extension as the test files. Next, we will add a section to our `package.json` file specifically to load the configuration for the `cucumber` plugin in our project and tell the plugin where to find our feature files:

```
"cypress-cucumber-preprocessor": {
  "nonGlobalStepDefinitions": true,
  "stepDefinitions": "./cypress/e2e"
}
```

In the preceding code, we added the necessary configuration code to our `package.json` file. Now that Cucumber is configured in our project, we will use it to write a test for the user flow of creating and deleting a blog post for the blog application previously introduced in the *Cypress-driven development* section. First, we will create a feature file:

```
Feature: Blog Application

  Scenario: A user can create a blog post.
    Given I am on the home page
    When I click the "New Post" link
    When I fill out the new blog form
    When I click "Submit"
    Then I see the new post on the home page
```

In the preceding code, we create a feature file for the scenario where a user creates a blog post. Next, we will write the associated code for the Gherkin steps:

```
import { Given, Then, When } from 'cypress-cucumber-
  preprocessor/steps'
import post from '../../support/generateBlogPost'
const currentPost = post
Given('I am on the home page', () => {
  cy.visit('/')
})


When('I click the "New Post" link', () => {
  cy.findByRole('link', { name: /new post/i }).click()
})
```

In the preceding code, first, we import the `Given`, `Then`, and `When` methods from the Cypress Cucumber library. Next, we import the fake `post` method to generate test data. Since each test step will live in its own method, we store the `fake post` data to maintain the same post throughout the test. Then, we use the `Given` method to create the first test step. The step name: `I am on the home page` must match the feature file's same words. Inside the `Given` method, we write the Cypress code associated with the step. Next, use the `When` method to create the next step. Next, we will add the following step definitions:

```
When('I fill out the new blog form', () => {
  cy.findByRole('textbox', { name: /title/i
```

```
  }).type(currentPost.title)
  cy.findByRole('textbox', { name: /category/i
  }).type(currentPost.category)
  cy.findByRole('textbox', { name: /image link/i
  }).type(currentPost.image_url)
  cy.findByRole('textbox', { name: /content/i
  }).type(currentPost.content)
})

When('I click "Submit"', () => {
  cy.findByRole('button', { name: /submit/i }).click()
})
```

In the preceding code, we used the When method to write the associated code for the I fill out the new blog form and I click "Submit" steps. Finally, we use the Then method to create the final step definition:

```
Then('I see the new post on the home page', () => {
  cy.findByRole('link', { name: currentPost.title
  }).should('be.visible')
})
```

In the preceding code, we use the Then method to create the associated code for the I see the new post on the home page step. We will create a Cucumber test for the *delete a blog post* user flow for the next test.

First, we make the Gherkin feature scenario:

```
  Scenario: A user can delete a blog post.
    Given I am on the home page
    When I click the blog post name link
    When I click the delete link
    Then the post is removed from the home page
```

In the preceding code, we create a scenario for deleting a blog post. Next, we will write the associated step definitions:

```
When('I click the blog post name link', () => {
  cy.findByRole('link', { name: currentPost.title
  }).click()
```

```
})
When('I click the delete link', () => {
    cy.findByText(/delete post>/i).click()
})
```

In the preceding code, we use the `When` method to add the associated test code for the `I click the blog post name link` and `I click the delete link` steps. Finally, we use the `Then` method to create the `the post is removed from the home page` step:

```
Then('the post is removed from the home page', () => {
    cy.findByRole('link', { name: currentPost.title
    }).should('not.exist')
})
```

In the preceding code, we add the test code associated with the last step to verify the deleted post is removed from the **Home** page. Notice that we didn't need to create another method for the `I am on the home page` step. Cucumber is smart enough to use any step definition that matches the string of text in the feature file.

Now you know how to write Gherkin-style tests in Cypress using Cucumber. You can do other things with Cucumber, such as adding tags to run specific tests and creating data tables that allow you to test multiple arguments for similar Gherkin steps.

Using React Developer Tools with Cypress

In the previous section, we learned how to write tests using Cucumber. In this section, we will learn how to install **React Developer Tools** for development. React Developer Tools is a great tool to have while developing React applications. It enables you to inspect the hierarchy of components rendered in the DOM and do things such as viewing and editing component props and state. There are Chrome and Firefox extensions available to install React Developer Tools. There is also a standalone Electron app version, which is useful, such as when you want to debug React applications in Safari or mobile browsers. We will also learn how to use the standalone version with Cypress.

Use the following command to install via the command line:

```
npm install --save-dev react-devtools
```

The preceding command will install `react-devtools` as a development dependency in your project. Next, we need to add a script that will connect `react-devtools` to your application. If you are building a Next.js application, install the special `<script src="http://localhost:8097">` script in the Head component in the _ `document.js` file:

```
<Head>
  <script src="http://localhost:8097"></script>
</Head>
```

In the preceding code, we added the script inside the Head component. The script ensures React Developer Tools connects to your Next.js application. If you are building an application using `create-react-app`, install the special script in the head element of the `index.html` file located in the `public` folder:

```
<!DOCTYPE html>
<html lang="en">
  <head>
    <script src="http://localhost:8097"></script>
```

In the preceding code, we add the script as the first thing inside the head element. We need to remember to remove the special `react-devtools` script before deploying the application to production because it is a development tool that would add unnecessary code to our production-versioned application.

After the script has been added, next we will create an npm script in the `package.json` file to start the tool:

```
"scripts": {
  "devtools": "react-devtools"
```

In the preceding code, we added a `devtools` script to run `react-devtools`. Now that we have a script to run the tool, the last thing we need to do is start our application, the Cypress interactive tool, and `react-devtools`: each in a separate tab at the command line.

For Next.js applications, use the following command:

```
npm run dev
```

We ran the preceding command to start the Next.js application in development. For `create-react-app` applications, use the following command:

```
npm start
```

We ran the preceding command to start the `create-react-app` application in development. In the *Getting started with Cypress* section, we created a `"cy:open"` script to start Cypress in interactive mode. We can run the script like so:

```
npm run cy:open
```

In the preceding command, we ran the script to start Cypress. The next thing we need to do is run the `react-devtools` script:

```
npm run devtools
```

In the preceding command, we ran the script to start `react-devtools`. When run, `react-devtools` opens its application on our computer:

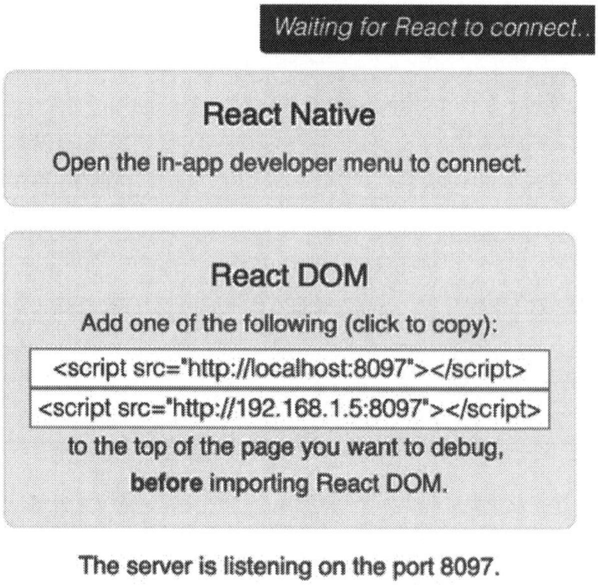

Figure 7.18 – React Developer Tools application

In the preceding screenshot, `react-devtools` opens and listens for our application to run to connect to it. Once we run any of our Cypress tests via the interactive mode, the applications component tree will populate inside of the `react-devtools` application:

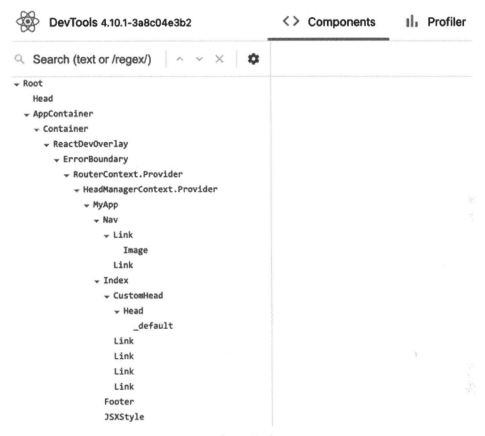

Figure 7.19 – React Developer Tools component tree view

In the preceding screenshot, the `react-devtools` application displays the resulting component tree of the running test. With the application running, we have many tools available, such as clicking on component names to view related information:

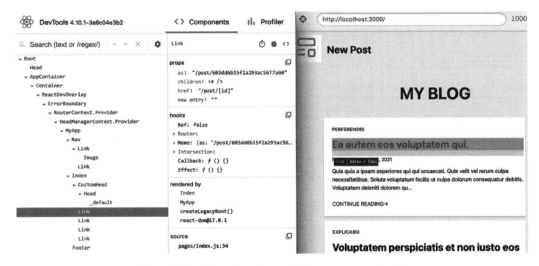

Figure 7.20 – React Developer Tools component details

In the preceding screenshot, we select one of the `Link` components on the left side of the `react-devtools` screen. When we click the component, it displays associated information on the `react-devtools` screen's right side, such as `props` and `hooks`. We also see the Cypress interactive mode screen on the right side of the screenshot.

Now you know how to use React Developer Tools with Cypress. In addition to the debugging tools provided by Cypress, you now have an extra tool to debug React applications while running Cypress.

Summary

In this chapter, you have learned new strategies to test applications using Cypress. You can write end-to-end tests to verify critical user flows for applications. You learned how to implement API testing. You now know the benefits of using Cypress-driven development to create new features. You understand the POM and custom command design patterns to structure and organize test code.

Finally, you learned how to use Cucumber to write Gherkin-style tests that enhance communication with non-technical team members.

Congratulations, you have reached the end of our journey and now know about numerous strategies and tools to simplify testing React applications! The concepts and skills gained in this book will help you write quality code no matter what JavaScript project you tackle in the future.

Good luck, and always remember, no great software is built without a foundation of great tests.

Questions

1. Find a previous project and install and write a suite of end-to-end tests with Cypress.

2. Create a CRUD API and test it using Cypress.

3. Build a full-stack React application and write as many tests as you can think of using as many different strategies gained from this book as possible.

Answers

Here you will find the answers to the questions provided at the end of each chapter:

Chapter 1

All questions are open-response.

Chapter 2

1. The **render** method.
2. The **screen** object.
3. Presentational components.
4. The **debug** method.
5. This is an open-response question.

Chapter 3

1. The **user-event** module closely resembles events that occur when users perform actions on the DOM, such as **keydown** and **keyup** events.
2. MSW allows you to test components that make HTTP requests to APIs. This is done by intercepting the request before it reaches the internet and instead returns controllable mock data for testing.
3. A mock function is a test double used to make assertions. For example, we can use a mock function to verify that a method is called when a user clicks a button.
4. The risk is that substituting actual dependencies with mocked versions to test components doesn't allow you to test resulting behaviors when integrated with real production dependencies.

5. This is an open-response question.

6. Use a getBy* query when you expect an element to be present in the DOM's current state. Use a findBy* query when an element's presence depends on an asynchronous action that delays the time the element appears in the DOM. Use a queryBy* query when you want to verify that an element is not present in the DOM.

Chapter 4

1. Testing integrated components allow you to mitigate risk by verifying production behavior when components interact with each other. Using the isolated approach, we would be replacing real dependencies with fake data and responses and, therefore, not mitigate as much risk. Also, in many situations, you can cover more code in fewer tests using the integrated testing approach.

2. You should only use the data-testid attribute as the last resort when other preferred queries methods such as getBy* and findBy* cannot be used to select elements.

3. The act method ensures your tests behave closer to how React updates the browser's DOM. Use act in situations where you need to manually make component updates such as resolving a Promise that React otherwise would not be aware of in your test. React Testing Library automatically wraps components in act eliminating the need to manually wrap all code that updates the component in most scenarios, such as click events.

Chapter 5

1. Unlike Enzyme or ReactTestUtils, React Testing Library allows you to write tests that avoid implementation details and resemble DOM interactions from the end user's perspective.

2. Running tests in Jest's Watch Mode allows you to learn when regressions occur as you add new code quickly. Running tests in Watch Mode is also beneficial when using the TDD approach to building components.

3. Use the each method when you want to execute the same test multiple times with different values.

Chapter 6

All questions are open-response.

Chapter 7

All questions are open-response.

Packt.com

Subscribe to our online digital library for full access to over 7,000 books and videos, as well as industry leading tools to help you plan your personal development and advance your career. For more information, please visit our website.

Why subscribe?

- Spend less time learning and more time coding with practical eBooks and Videos from over 4,000 industry professionals

- Improve your learning with Skill Plans built especially for you

- Get a free eBook or video every month

- Fully searchable for easy access to vital information

- Copy and paste, print, and bookmark content

Did you know that Packt offers eBook versions of every book published, with PDF and ePub files available? You can upgrade to the eBook version at packt.com and as a print book customer, you are entitled to a discount on the eBook copy. Get in touch with us at customercare@packtpub.com for more details.

At www.packt.com, you can also read a collection of free technical articles, sign up for a range of free newsletters, and receive exclusive discounts and offers on Packt books and eBooks.

Other Books You May Enjoy

If you enjoyed this book, you may be interested in these other books by Packt:

UI Testing with Puppeteer

Dario Kondratiuk

ISBN: 978-1-80020-678-6

- Understand browser automation fundamentals
- Explore end-to-end testing with Puppeteer and its best practices
- Apply CSS Selectors and XPath expressions to web automation
- Discover how you can leverage the power of web automation as a developer
- Emulate different use cases of Puppeteer such as network speed tests and geolocation
- Get to grips with techniques and best practices for web scraping and web content generation

End-to-End Web Testing with Cypress

Waweru Mwaura

ISBN: 978-1-83921-385-4

- Get to grips with Cypress and understand its advantages over Selenium
- Explore common Cypress commands, tools, and techniques for writing complete tests for web apps
- Set up and configure Cypress for cross-browser testing
- Understand how to work with elements and animation to write non-flaky tests
- Discover techniques for implementing and handling navigation requests in tests
- Implement visual regression tests with Applitools eyes

Packt is searching for authors like you

If you're interested in becoming an author for Packt, please visit authors. packtpub.com and apply today. We have worked with thousands of developers and tech professionals, just like you, to help them share their insight with the global tech community. You can make a general application, apply for a specific hot topic that we are recruiting an author for, or submit your own idea.

Leave a review - let other readers know what you think

Please share your thoughts on this book with others by leaving a review on the site that you bought it from. If you purchased the book from Amazon, please leave us an honest review on this book's Amazon page. This is vital so that other potential readers can see and use your unbiased opinion to make purchasing decisions, we can understand what our customers think about our products, and our authors can see your feedback on the title that they have worked with Packt to create. It will only take a few minutes of your time, but is valuable to other potential customers, our authors, and Packt. Thank you!

Index

W

Printed in Great Britain
by Amazon

63793707R00140